Assessing and Mitigating Business Risks in India

Assessing and Mitigating Business Risks in India

Balbir B. Bhasin

business**expert**
Press

Assessing and Mitigating Business Risks in India
Copyright © Business Expert Press, 2012.

First published in 2012 by
Business Expert Press, LLC
222 East 46th Street, New York, NY 10017
www.businessexpertpress.com

ISBN-13: 978-1-60649-312-0 (paperback)

ISBN-13: 978-1-60649-313-7 (e-book)

DOI 10.4128/9781606493137

Business Expert Press International Business collection

Collection ISSN: 1948-2752 (print)
Collection ISSN: 1948-2760 (electronic)

Cover design by Jonathan Pennell
Interior design by Exeter Premedia Services Private Ltd.,
Chennai, India

First edition: 2012

10 9 8 7 6 5 4 3 2 1

Printed in the United States of America.

Abstract

This book focusses on the business opportunities India offers the world. Even as it draws attention to the challenges and risks involved in doing business in India, it provides suggestions for overcoming them. It begins by providing a background to understanding India and sets the stage by highlighting the business environment in which the economic, legal, and cultural variances exist. This is necessary to understand the complexity that exists in India. Potential markets are then discussed, focusing on the sectors, regions, and cities where growth is taking place; the upper, middle, and lower income segments; Indian multinational enterprises (MNEs); public sector and state-owned companies, and family-owned enterprises. This is followed by an overview of the various pitfalls and obstacles that are frequently encountered when operating in India, including political uncertainty and intransigence, corruption, bureaucratic roadblocks, the web of litigation, protecting intellectual property (IP), labor and human resources limitations, and India's ubiquitous second economy. These not only increase risk and lead to costly delays on account of lengthy litigation and payment of bribes, aggravating frustration, but also result in total loss of investments. The book provides keys to success, including guidelines for selecting partners and appointing agents, as well as negotiating techniques that work in India. Finally, the book provides a comprehensive list of web resources to help the reader explore further, and connect with government and private sector bodies.

Keywords

India, South Asia, South Asian Association for Regional Cooperation (SAARC), South Asian Free Trade Agreement (SAFTA), Asian cultures, business opportunities, business strategy, cross-cultural communications, doing business in Asia, emerging markets, foreign direct investment (FDI), global business, global strategy, technology transfer, international trade, international management, international marketing, international marketing research

Contents

Introduction

India is a major economic force in the global economy. Its growth rate has been nothing short of stupendous. In 2010, its annual growth was 8.75% and is expected to increase to 9–10% for each of the next 10 years. It has been estimated that India's current gross domestic product (GDP) is already $3.8 trillion (on a public and private partnership (PPP) basis), placing it on par with Japan. By 2013, it may become the third largest economy after the United States and China.

India offers tremendous opportunities for investment and business. It is a thriving democracy. It has a capitalist economy that has a high savings rate, which accounts for 37% of the gross domestic product (GDP). India has a large talent pool that is English speaking. Its massive population is young (average age is 25) and well educated. It has a fast-emerging middle class of perhaps 200 million with a propensity for increased consumption. The wealthiest consumers who earn $1 million or more (in PPP terms) will total 40 million in the next 10 years. Private sector participation is increasing and India has 45 million entrepreneurs. India's legal framework remains a model for many emerging economies. The financial system is well regulated. This allowed it to weather the recent global financial crisis. India's banking sector is strong, with impressive balance sheets. India is the leading global source in knowledge and business processing services. The country has an immediate need for infrastructure development. Ample participation opportunities exist in manufacturing, service, and technology sectors. India needs capital to expand as well as update its technology. The government of India has taken numerous initiatives to attract foreign investment in diverse sectors by offering incentives and reducing tariffs, licenses, and other red tape.

Yet, India is a "love it or hate it" country with great potential but one that no one pretends is easy to maneuver. The World Bank rates India 134th out of 183 countries for "Ease of Doing Business" while China is ranked 89th, the United States fourth, and Singapore first. The report takes into account areas such as starting a business, dealing with construction permits, registering property, getting credit, protecting investors, paying taxes, trading across borders, enforcing contracts, closing a business, getting electricity, and employing workers.

Development in India has been uneven, with some parts of the country showing spectacular growth while others are seriously lagging behind. Challenges exist in the areas of food production and distribution as well as power generation. The country suffers on account of inadequate infrastructure, government monopolies and inefficiencies, failing education, endemic corruption, inflation, and, most of all, impediments created by a cumbersome bureaucracy. The Indian business environment is amorphous, with conditions varying from state to state, region to region, and industry to industry. These are risks that require well-informed assessment and mitigation, which this book explores and endeavors to address.

CHAPTER 1

Background: The Complexity that is India

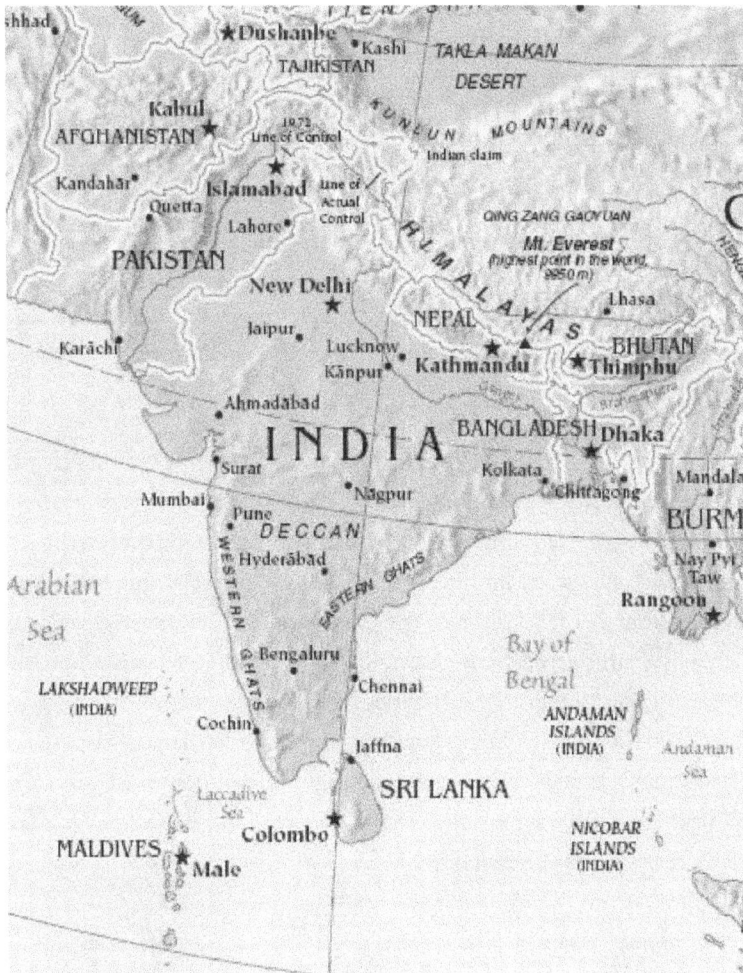

Country at a Glance

Size	3,287,263 sq km (slightly more than a third of the size of the United States)
Climate	Tropical monsoon in the south and temperate in the north
Capital	New Delhi
Political structure	Sovereign, socialist, secular, democratic republic
Leader	Prime Minister Manmohan Singh
Official languages	Hindi, Bengali, Telugu, Tamil, Urdu, Gujarati, Marathi, Malayalam, Kannada, Oriya, Punjabi, Assamese, Kashmiri, Sindhi, and Sanskrit
Other languages spoken	English is a subsidiary official language
Population	1,189,172,906 (July 2011 est.)
Age breakdown	0–14 (29.7%), 15–64 (64.9%), 65+ (5.5%)
Major religion	Hindu (80.5%)
Other religions	Islam (13.4%), Christianity (2.3%), Sikhism (1.9%), others (0.1%)
Major industries	Textiles, chemicals, food processing, steel, transportation equipment, cement, mining, petroleum, machinery, software, pharmaceuticals
GDP	$4,463 trillion (2011 est.)
GDP per capita	$3,700 (2011 est.)

Note. Adapted from Central Intelligence Agency: The World Factbook 2011a. Retrieved February 18, 2012, from https://www.cia.gov/library/publications/the-world-factbook/geos/in.html

India's complexity is astounding, with its long and winding history, huge population, diverse cultures, great ancient and contemporary religions and yet a secular state, multitude of ethnic languages, unique geographic regions from the Himalayas to the plains and the oceans, wide array of rich and confusing customs and traditions, plethora of castes and social hierarchies and economic disparities with formal positive and negative discrimination, and political plurality in the world's largest democracy. The contrasts in India can give much insight into understanding its complexity. The following report in the *New York Times* illustrates the paradoxes that exist in contemporary India:

> *In this city [Gurgaon] that barely existed two decades ago, there are*
> *26 shopping malls, seven golf courses and luxury shops selling Chanel*

and Louis Vuitton. Mercedes-Benz and BMWs shimmer in automobile showrooms. Apartment towers are sprouting like concrete weeds, and a futuristic commercial hub called Cyber City houses many of the world's most respected corporations.

Located about 15 miles south of the national capital, New Delhi, Gurgaon would seem to have everything, except consider what it does not have: a functioning citywide sewer or drainage system; reliable electricity or water; and public sidewalks, adequate parking, decent roads or any citywide system of public transportation. Garbage is still regularly tossed in empty lots by the side of the road.[1]

In order to appreciate the unique and exceptional environment of India, it is necessary to understand the fundamentals of the country— its history, geography, demographics, and political, economic, legal, and social environment—that have made it what it is today. This chapter lays out these fundamentals as a prelude to discussing the opportunities and risks of doing business in India.

Indian Past: A Great Civilization

India is one of the oldest of the world's great civilizations. According to Pulitzer Prize winning author and scientist Jared Diamond, the Indian and Chinese civilizations can be traced back to over a million years ago, whereas the European civilization has a history that is half as old. From its African origin at around 7 million BC, humanity spread to the Fertile Crescent and then to India and China in 1 million BC. Diamond includes the Indian subcontinent as part of greater Eurasia, while China is the mainstay of the East Asian evolution that ultimately spread southward to Southeast Asia, the Pacific Islands, and Australia, as well as northwards across the Bering Straits to the Arctic and subsequently to all of the North and South American continents.[2] Both India and China have contributed much to human evolution. From India came wheat, barley, sorghum, hyacinth bean, black and green gram, cotton, flax, and cucumber. This is not to say that the Fertile Crescent made little contribution; as a matter of fact the early civilization in what is today Iraq, Iran, and Turkey discovered emmer wheat, einkorn wheat, barley, pea, lentil, chickpea, flax, and muskmelon. From India came the three great Asian religions of Jainism, Hinduism, and Buddhism, as well as the discovery of the numeral zero, chess, astronomy, astrology, dyes, and colors. India and China also contributed to language expansion in the old world, as well as an amazing variety of musical instruments, and more recently an array of spices and foods.[3]

India's earliest civilization dates back to around the third millennium BC when the local Dravidians inhabited the Indus Valley, from which the name India is derived. Physically they were shorter, darker skinned people, proto-Australoids, and akin to the aborigines of South and Southeastern Asia. This urban society was highly organized. Its script has yet to be deciphered.

The Indus Valley Civilization ended abruptly around 1800 BC with the influx of new people to India. These were mainly nomadic tribes from Central Asia. These are referred to as Aryans or Indo-Europeans. It is believed that each wave moved southwards, intermingling and displacing the Dravidians. Eventually, the Dravidians, who were mostly in the west, south, and east were overrun by the warlike Aryans but in the process became localized. Aryan and Dravidian cultures merged and a new civilization began to surface. The four Vedas - great books of knowledge in Sanskrit—were written between 1500 BC and 1000 BC. Socioeconomic divisions that existed within the society during this time resulted in the hierarchical stratification of society known as the caste system.

The next great invasion into India occurred from Persia around 500 BC. The Persians occupied the Indus Valley for about 150 years. Then came the Greeks under Alexander in 326 BC but they left behind only a garrison and did not move beyond the northwest. Aryan-based kingdoms continued to flourish independently in the east and expanded to the north as the Maurya dynasty. Emperor Ashoka (268–231 BC) ruled as far south as Mysore and supported the spread of Buddhism through Asia. The Mauryan dynasty lasted a mere 100 years.

The Greeks under King Menander came again in 150 BC and occupied a small part of the north, but the local kingdoms enjoyed relative autonomy for the next four hundred years or so. In 319 AD, the Gupta dynasty emerged, which ruled the entire north and as far south as the Vindhya mountains for 150 years. Then, six thriving and separate kingdoms covering most of India allowed for relative stability (termed the Golden Age of art) until the dawn of the Muslim era.

Arab traders had been visiting the western coast since 712 AD but it was only in 1001 AD that a series of Arab armies swept down the Khyber Pass to wreak havoc, pillage, and plunder. The first Muslim invader who stayed came in 1192. He was Mohammed of Ghor and by 1202 he had conquered most of the powerful Hindu kingdoms along the River Ganga. The Sultanate of Delhi was established in 1202. It ruled over the north while the south remained free of invaders. However, in 1397 Mongol hordes under Tamerlane invaded from Samarkand and ravaged the entire region. It was only in 1527 that the Mughals (Persian for Mongol) under Babur came to power. The Mughals ruled India until their disintegration in the early 18th century.

The arrival of the Europeans began with the Portuguese trading in Goa as early as 1510, and beginning in 1610 the British East India Company slowly started consolidating its hold over the entire subcontinent. The rule was to last 300 years, as the British divided the country into governable districts using local rulers as proxies.[4] It was only after the Second World War and the decline of the British Empire that India emerged as a sovereign state in 1947 when the country was partitioned

Event	Date	Description
Dravidians	3000 BC	Dravidians inhabited the indus valley, from which the name India is deriveda
Aryans	1800 BC	Influx of new people, mainly normadic tribes from Central Asia
Dravidians localized	1500–1000 BC	Aryan and Dravidian cultures merged. Presumedly, four great books of knowledge (Vedas) written in Sanskrit. Beginning of the caste system
Invasion from Persia	500 BC	Persian occupied Indus valley for 150 years
Invasion by Alexander the great	326 BC	Left behind a garrison but did not move northwest. Aryan based kingdoms continued to flourish
Emperor Ashoka	268–231 BC	Maurya dynasty lasted 100 years. Spread of Buddhism
Invasion by King Menander	150 BC	Greeks occupied the north. Local kingdoms enjoyed autonomy for 400 years
Emergence of Guptas	AD 319	Guptas dynasty emerged. Also termed as "Golden Age of Art"
Arab traders	712 AD	By 1001 AD, Arabs armies swept down the Khyber pass to wreck havoc, pillage and plunder
Invasion by Mohammad of Ghor	1192–1202	Conquered the most powerful hindu kingdoms along the Ganges
Mughal under Babur	1527	Mughal under Babur ruled for till early 18th century
Arrival of Europeans	1510	Portugese trading began in Goa. Consolidation of British East India Company. British ruled for 300 years
India Independence	1947	Became a soverign state. Hindu majority became India and Muslim majority became Pakistan

Figure 1.1. Timeline of India.

into two states - Hindu majority India and a Muslim majority Pakistan. Modern India is secular and encompasses the legacies of Hindu, Buddhist, Muslim, Sikh, and Christian empires.

Geography: The South Asian Subcontinent

India occupies most of the subcontinent of Southern Asia. In size, India is the seventh largest country in the world. It is a third of the size of the United States. Land area is 3.29 million square kilometers (1.27 million square miles). India measures 3,214 km (1,997 miles) from north to south and 2,993 km (1,860 miles) from east to west. It stretches eastwards from Pakistan to Bangladesh and Myanmar (Burma). China, Nepal, and Bhutan are to the north. In the far south lie the islands of Sri Lanka and Indonesia. The Indian Ocean lies to its south, the Arabian Sea to its west and the Bay of Bengal to the east. Lakshadweep Islands (a total of 36) are in the Arabian Sea and the Andaman and Nicobar Islands (a total of 572) in the Bay of Bengal.[5]

India consists of three distinct geographic regions. First is the Himalayan region in the north where some of the highest mountains in the world are located. The Indo-Gangetic Plain, which lies to the northeast, is watered by three great rivers, the Indus, the Ganga, and the Brahmaputra. Its highly fertile soil has drawn millions of people, making it among the most populous regions in the world. Finally, the central region and the southern peninsula consist of the Deccan plateau and the coastal plains.

Climate in India varies significantly across the regions. It ranges from biting cold and snowfall in the mountains of the north to a tropical climate in the south. There are four seasons: winter, when it is dry and cool (from December to February); summer, when it is dry and hot (from March to May); monsoons, when it rains (from June to September) and post-monsoon, when the dry monsoons retreat. Average temperatures range from 12–30°C in the northwest, 17–30°C in the north and northeast, and 22–30°C in the south. Winters in peninsular India are mostly mild but it is much cooler in the north.[6]

India is endowed with numerous natural resources. It has the third or fourth largest coal reserves in the world. Mineral deposits include iron ore (fourth largest producer in the world), mica (world's biggest producer),

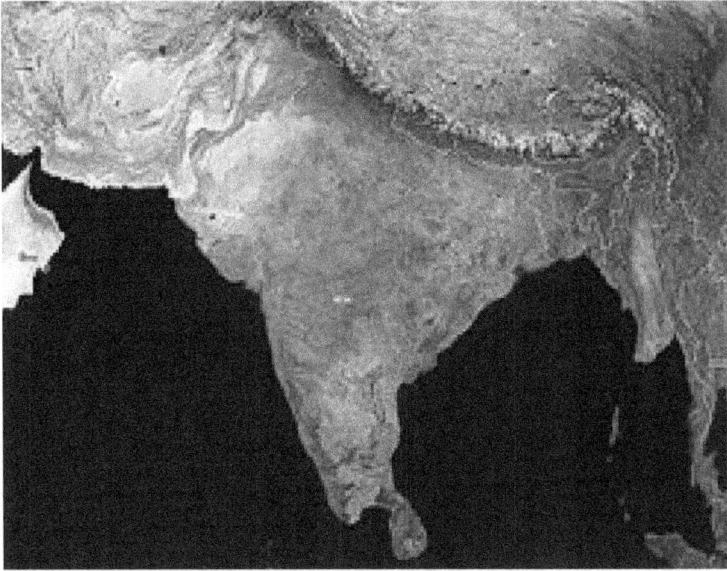

Source: Adapted from Wikipedia 2011a. Retrieved July 20, 2011, from http://en.wikipedia.org/wiki/Geography_of_India

barite and chromite (second in the world), bauxite (fifth largest), manganese (seventh largest), rare earth elements, titanium ore, diamonds, and limestone. India also has petroleum reserves of about 5.4 million barrels and 17 trillion cubic feet of natural gas reserves. Fifty-six percent of India's land is arable and used for agriculture.[7]

Demographics: An Extremely Diverse Nation

India has the second largest population in the world after China, estimated to be 1.2 billion (July 2011). Thirty percent of the total population lives in cities and urbanization is growing at 2.4% annually. The major cities and population in millions are: Delhi 22, Mumbai 20, Kolkata 15, Chennai 7.5, Bangalore 7, Hyderabad 6, and Ahmedabad 5.5. India has a 61% literacy rate (those who are 15 years and older and can read and write). Of the literate, 73% are male and 48% female.

In terms of ethnicity, 72% of the population is Indo-Aryan, 25% Dravidian, and 3% Mongoloid and other. Around 80.5% of the population is Hindu, 13.4% Muslim, 2.3% Christian, 1.9% Sikh, and 1.8% Buddhist,

Jain, Parsi, and others or unspecified (2001 census). India has a multitude of languages. The Indian census lists 114 languages (22 of which are spoken by one million or more persons). Hindi is spoken by about 41% of the population. There are 216 "mother tongues" that are spoken by 10,000 or more people. An estimated 850 languages are in daily use and the Indian Government reports that there are more than 1,600 dialects. Regional officially recognized languages are: Bengali (8.1%), Telugu (7.2%), Marathi (7%), Tamil (5.9%), Urdu (5%), Gujarati (4.5%), Kannada (3.7%), Malayalam (3.2%), Oriya (3.2%), Punjabi (2.8%), Assamese (1.3%), Maithili (1.2%), and others (5.9%). English has an official status and is widely used in business and politics.[8]

The majority of the population (65%) is in the 15–64 years age group, 30% are between 0 and 14 years and the older segment of 65 years and beyond constitutes about 5%. The median age is thus only 26.2 years, making India a country with a rather young population. Population growth rate is 1.34% (86th in the world). Birth rate is 20.97 births per 1,000 (ranking 84th). The gender ratio is 1.08 males for every female. Life expectancy is 66 years - 161st in the world. Total fertility rate is 2.62 children born per woman - ranked at 79th in the world.[9]

Business Environment: Political, Economic, and Legal

Political System

India is a "sovereign, socialist, secular, democratic republic" as stipulated in its constitution. It is based on the heavily amended 1950 Constitution, which provides for a federal form of government, much like the United States.[10] A major difference is that India's central government (also known as the union government) has greater power in relation to its states. Its structure is much like the British parliamentary system, with distinct, but interrelated executive, legislative, and judicial branches. State governments are structured similarly to the central government and district governments exist in a variety of forms.[11]

The president is the head of state while the prime minister is the head of government. Executive power of the government lies with the cabinet (senior members of the council of ministers) led by the prime minister, who is selected by legislators of the political party or coalition commanding a majority in the *Lok Sabha* (lower house). The prime minister is officially appointed by the president and in turn recommends to him the appointment of subordinate ministers. The president and vice president are mainly ceremonial posts and are elected indirectly for a 5-year term by a special electoral college. Their terms are staggered and the vice president does not automatically become president if the president dies or is removed from office.[12]

The legislative branch consists of the *Rajya Sabha* (council of states) and the *Lok Sabha* (house of the people). The council of ministers is responsible to the Lok Sabha. It has 545 seats, out of which 543 are elected by popular vote and 2 are appointed by the president. Members serve 5-year terms. The Rajya Sabha has 233 members elected from the states and union territories, and the president appoints another 12 making a total of 245. They serve 6-year terms with one third coming up for election every 2 years. The legislature passes laws on constitutionally specified matters.

The Judicial branch consists of the Supreme Court, which has a chief justice and 25 associate justices, all appointed by the president on the advice of the prime minister. They remain in office till the age of 65 or if removed for "proved misbehavior." The Indian judicial system is said to be very independent.

India has 28 states and 7 union territories including the national capital territory of New Delhi. States and union territories contain 601 districts that are further subdivided into townships containing 200–600 villages. State government legislatures are either bicameral or unicameral and the elected chief minister functions at the state level much like the prime minister at the national level. Each state also has a governor appointed by the president of India. They may assume certain broad powers when directed by the central government. The central government exerts greater authority over the union territories and local governments in India have less autonomy than do the states in the United States. Many states still retain the traditional village councils *(Panchayats)* to address local matters through democratic participation. Over half-a-million panchayats exist throughout India. To ensure political representation for historically marginalized groups in the lower house of parliament, the Indian Constitution stipulates that each state reserve seats for Scheduled

Castes and Scheduled Tribes in proportion to their population in the state. This means only candidates belonging to these groups can contest elections in reserved constituencies. In the 2009 elections, 84 seats for candidates from Scheduled Castes and 47 for Scheduled Tribe members were reserved, 24% of the total seats in the parliament's lower house.

In its foreign relations, India has participated considerably in world affairs and has taken pride as a leader in the Non-Aligned Movement (NAM). Today, India's economic, military, and scientific and technological strength has allowed it to become more assertive. It is seeking a permanent seat on the Security Council of the United Nations (UN) and has been an active member and a leading contributor in UN peacekeeping operations. With the end of the cold war, India has strengthened its relations with the US, Japan, the European Union (EU), Iran, China, and the Association of South East Asian Nations (ASEAN). It remains an active member of the South Asian Association for Regional Cooperation (SAARC).[13]

India is the world's largest democracy but political stability remains a dream unfulfilled. There are almost 1,000 political parties, mostly regional operatives. This has led to an era of coalition politics in recent decades. Coalitions led by either the Indian National Congress (INC) or the Bharatiya Janata Party (BJP) have dominated federal-level politics. In the 64 years since India's independence, the INC has ruled for 51 of those years. The dispersed nature of politics at the federal level has led to a need to govern through compromise. This is further exacerbated by endemic corruption at most levels, which is not limited to buying votes. Differing demands from states and constituencies severely limit the central government's ability to enforce much-needed policies. Many of these parties are race, caste, language, religion, and region based. There continues to be a struggle between secular (Congress, Communists) and religion-based parties (BJP and its adjunct RSS). The socialist legacy of the past has also left an entrenched labor movement, which is very organized and active politically. Its activism has often led to violence. A uniquely Indian form of labor protests is the *bandh* (literally closure and similar to a strike) and it is widely used to achieve political ends.

A recent dynamic shift in the political system has been the devolution of political power from the federal and state levels right down to the villages under the innovative traditional institution of the *panchayat*. It involves 250,000 elected institutions of local self-government, with 3.2 million elected members of whom 1.2 million are women. Another is the newly enacted "Right to Information Act," which enables citizens to seek information on the reasons or background of any executive decision of the government. This is expected to have a pronounced effect on transparency and governance.

Economic System

India is slowly developing into an open market economy but many impediments still exist. From independence in 1947 to the late 1970s, the Indian economy functioned as a centrally-planned system with import substitution and domestic-industrial production being the mainstay of the economy. Liberalization began rather slowly in the 1980s and it was only in 1991 that market-oriented reforms began in earnest. These included privatization of state-owned enterprises, reduction in control of foreign trade, liberalization of foreign investment and foreign exchange, reduction in tariffs and other trade barriers, opening and modernization of the financial sector, and overall adjustment of monetary and fiscal policies, and protection of intellectual property rights (IPRs).[14]

Today India is the 12th largest economy in the world and the third largest in Asia after China and Japan with total GDP exceeding $1.43 trillion ($3.8 trillion on a PPP basis). Growth has averaged in excess of 7% per annum since 1997 and India has managed to reduce poverty by about 10%. India's diverse economy encompasses traditional village farming, modern agriculture, numerous modern industries, and a multitude of services. The agricultural sector accounts for 18.1% of GDP, industry for 26.3%, and the services sector 55.6% (2011). India has a labor force of about 480 million (second largest in the world). Agriculture still employs 52% of the labor force, while industry and services employ 14% and 34%, respectively. Unemployment in India hovers at around 10.8% (118th in the world), the population living below the poverty line is estimated to be 25% (2009), and inflation is around 11.7% (2010). The country's per capita GDP (PPP) was $3,339 (129th) in 2010.

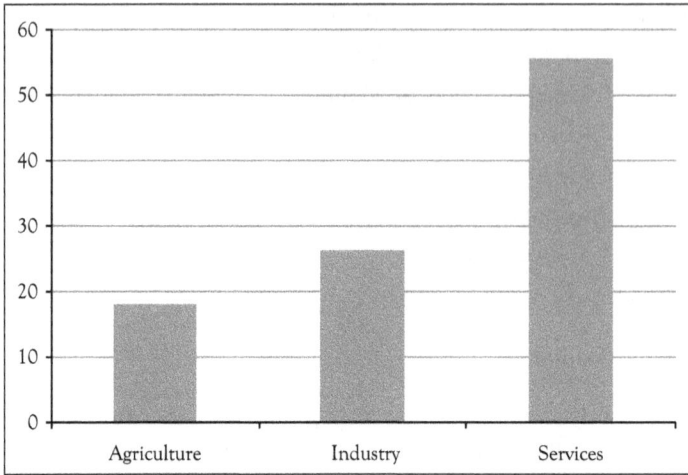

Figure 1.2. GDP by sector.

Source: Adapted from Central Intelligence Agency, The World Factbook, 2011 (data compiled from The World Factbook, 2011). Retrieved February 18, 2012, from https://www.cia.gov/library/publications/the-world-factbook/geos/in.html

With regard to farm output India ranks second in the world. Its agricultural produce includes rice, wheat, oilseed, cotton, jute, tea, sugarcane, lentils, onions, potatoes, dairy products, sheep, goats, poultry, and fish. Industries in India are: textiles, jute, chemicals, food processing, steel, transportation equipment, cement, aluminum, mining, petroleum, machinery, software, and pharmaceuticals. Indian exports are valued at $201 billion (2010) and include petroleum, precious stones, machinery, iron and steel, chemicals, tea, vehicles and vehicle parts, and apparel. India's main export partners are UAE (13%), the United States (13%), and China (6%). Imports valued at $327 billion include crude oil, precious stones, machinery, fertilizer, iron and steel, and chemicals. India's import partners are China (11%), the United States (7%), Saudi Arabia (5%), UAE (5%), Australia (5%), Germany (5%), and Singapore (4%). India's total trade (counting exports and imports) stands at $606.7 billion and is currently the 11th largest in the world.[15]

Until liberalization in 1991, foreign trade and foreign direct investment (FDI) were limited and restricted as India attempted to achieve self-sufficiency after having been exploited by foreigners for centuries. This was in spite of the fact that India was a founding member of the General

(A) Imports

(B) Exports

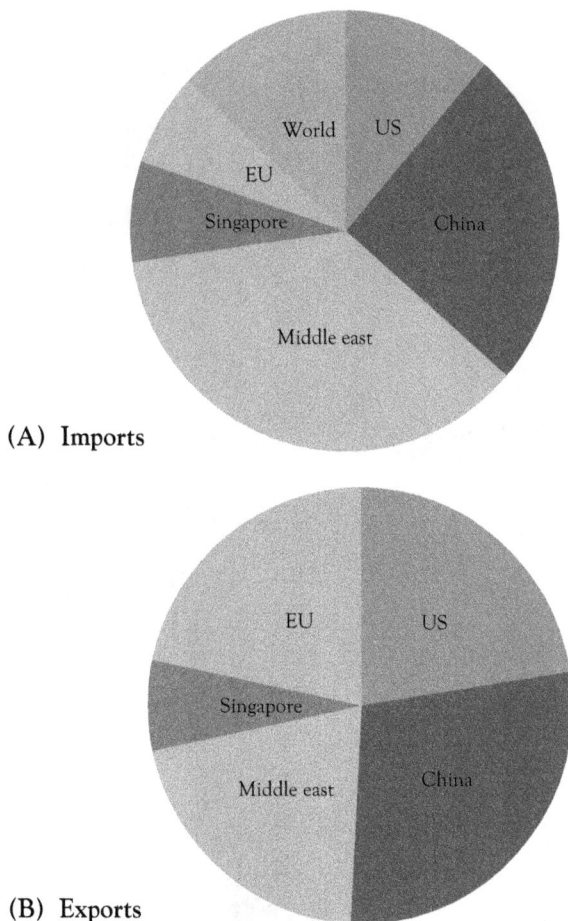

Figure 1.3. Major trading partners.

Source: Adapted from Asian Development Bank, 2011 (data compiled from Asian Development Bank 2011). Retrieved February 18, 2012, from http://www.adb.org/Documents/Books/Key_Indicators/2011/pdf/IND.pdf

Agreement on Trade and Tariffs (GATT), which is now the World Trade Organization (WTO). Foreign portfolio and FDI inflows have been increasing steadily in recent years, with Mauritius, Singapore, the United States, the United Kingdom, and the Netherlands being the main sources of FDI. The exceptionally high investment from Mauritius is due to routing of international funds through that country because of tax advantages. India now allows up to 100% FDI stake in certain ventures.

(A) Imports

(B) Exports

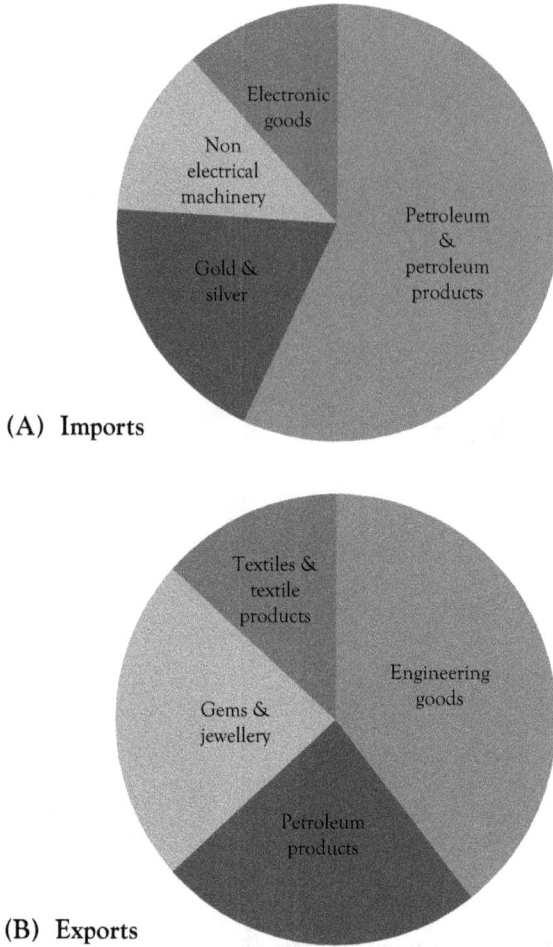

Figure 1.4. Major products traded.

Source: Adapted from Business without Borders. Country Briefing 2011a (data compiled from Global Opportunity Tool). Retrieved February 25, 2012, from http://country.eiu.com/article.asp x?articleid=218773406&Country=India& topic=Summary&subtopic=Fact+sheet&subsubtopic =Fact+sheet

India is signatory to the following free trade agreements: SAARC Preferential Trade Agreement, India–Singapore Comprehensive Economic Cooperation Agreement (CECA), ASEAN–India FTA, the CECA with Malaysia, and the recently concluded agreement with Japan. It is also negotiating Regional Trade Agreements with the EU and the Gulf Cooperation Council and FTAs with Australia, New Zealand, Egypt, South

Africa, Uruguay, and others. In total, India has 33 FTAs, which are at different stages of development - 11 in effect, one signed, 12 under negotiation, and nine under review.

India has become the leader in the business process outsourcing (BPO) industry thanks to its large pool of educated, English speaking, and software-trained personnel. This and industrial productivity have helped build a middle class which is growing exponentially. However, 700 million people live on $2 or less per day, mostly engaged in subsistence agriculture in rural areas. Economic growth is constrained by inadequate infrastructure, a cumbersome bureaucracy, corruption, labor market rigidities, and still to be reformed government controls.[16] The informal economy accounts for approximately 23% of the Gross National Income (GNI).[17]

Legal System

India's legal system is derived from English common law. The Indian Constitution contains civil liberties called "Fundamental Rights" that are guaranteed to all citizens. These include equality before the law and freedoms of speech, expression, religion, and association. Freedom of the press is not explicitly stated but is widely interpreted as included in the freedoms of speech and expression. However, the government has the power to limit civil liberties so as to preserve law and order as well as protect national security. There is no trial by jury and cases are decided by judges. The judiciary enforces the right to fair trial and there are channels to appeal against court decisions. Defendants can choose counsel independent of government and free counsel is provided for those that cannot afford one.[18]

The Supreme Court is the top legal entity. It has appellate jurisdiction over all civil and criminal proceedings as well as in the interpretation of the Constitution. Below the Supreme Court are high courts followed by a hierarchy of subordinate courts. Some high courts (totaling 21) serve more than one state, and all are independent of state legislators and executives. Besides the broad three-tiered courts, there are various specialized tribunals - the more prominent ones being the Company Law Board, Monopolies and Restrictive Trade Practices Commission, Consumer Protection Forum, Debts Recovery Tribunal, and the Tax Tribunal. These tribunals function under the supervisory jurisdiction of the High Court where they may be situated, though many of them (like the Monopolies Commission) allow an appeal directly to the Supreme Court.

The Indian judiciary is slow but highly respected for protecting citizens' rights. Indian courts have large backlogs. The backlog is a serious impediment to the efficient conduct of judicial proceedings in the country. Corruption is also rampant in India's courts. According to Transparency International, judicial corruption in India is attributable to factors such as "delays in the disposal of cases, shortage of judges and complex procedures, all of which are exacerbated by a preponderance of new laws."

Sociocultural Environment

India is one of the world's most ethnically diverse countries. Its ethnic and linguistic diversity is unlike that of any other nation-state and greater than that of all of Europe. Within the subcontinent are a large number of regional, social, and economic groups, each with different cultural practices. The nation's identity is a unique blend of cultures, religions, races, and languages. India is the birthplace of Buddhism, Hinduism, Jainism, and Sikhism.[19] There are three major written scripts, the Devanagari, Bengali, and Pallavi and they originate from the Brahmani script.

India is officially a secular country but the majority of the people practice Hinduism and religion rules every facet of life. Today it is practiced by more than 80% of the population. More than 12% of the population is Muslim; the world's third largest after Indonesia and Pakistan. Other religions include Sikhism (2%), Buddhism (0.8%), Jainism (0.4%), and a smaller number adhere to Christianity, Judaism, and Zoroastrianism. Hinduism, Buddhism, and Jainism have an ascetic heritage and this has resulted in the majority taking a mystical approach to life. There is a tendency to cultivate a culture of preparation for the hereafter.

India is famous for its complex social systems, perhaps unknown elsewhere. Indians belong to thousands of castes and caste-like groups that are part of a hierarchical ordering system. Within Indian culture all people are ranked according to various essential qualities such as north and south, rural and urban, wealth, power, education, religion, families and kinships, age, and gender. Each person has a fixed place in the social hierarchy that lasts throughout the lifetime and many even live on the fringes of these established structures. To say that Indian society is divided in a multitude of ways would be an understatement.[20]

The Hindu caste system has four major categories *(varnas)* that are subdivided further into *jatis*. Similar hereditary and occupational social hierarchies exist within the Sikh and Muslim communities as well, but are less pervasive and institutionalized. *Dalits* or "untouchables" constitute about 16% of the total population and are officially termed Scheduled Castes. Eight percent are termed Scheduled Tribes, which are the 461 indigenous groups, more commonly known as *adivasi*.[21] Although the practice of untouchability is outlawed it continues to be practiced across the country. It is more prevalent in rural India. Hindus especially have a fundamental belief in reincarnation. Each soul can be reincarnated for a number of rebirths that are determined by one's sins and good deeds. This belief provides justification for the inequities of the caste system.

British rule only served to strengthen the division by classes. Elitism, feudalism, and class values were strengthened as institutions based on bureaucracy, hierarchy, and subjugation were established and this legacy continues. Inequality already in place due to the caste system has deepened with the class structure widening the gap between the rich and the poor.

India is principally a *collectivist* culture. A strong sense of community prevails nationwide and group orientation is inbuilt into society. People rely on each other for financial and moral support. They are very deferential to group structures and hierarchy is accepted easily. Each individual knows his or her place in society. Privacy is not much respected and many questions of a personal nature are often asked. Personal space too is kept at a minimum. Respect for the elderly as well as for those of higher social standing is mandatory. Elders and those senior in position are respected and obeyed. Religious festivals and occasions are very important to Indians. Some of these celebrations are long-drawn-out affairs. People tend to show deference to religious figures and government officials. The Constitution of India gives equal rights to men and women in all walks of life but one cannot say that all women in India enjoy equal rights with men in all matters. There are many reasons for this: the customs and traditions prevalent for centuries; the unchecked male domination in all walks of life; the high percentage of illiteracy among women; the mainly patriarchal structure of society; and the acceptance of the theory of *karma* or fatalism. Indians are very loyal to their families and elders. The joint family system still prevails and taking care of elderly parents is seen as a filial duty.

The accepted form of greeting in India's business circles is a handshake, though *Namaste or Namaskar* (salutations or greetings; literally "I bow to you") is also used. This involves bringing both the palms together at chest level with a slight bow of the head. Traditional women may not shake hands but will greet you with folded hands. Indian men too may not shake hands with foreign women out of respect. Many men and especially women are uncomfortable with touching, such as a casual hug or a peck on the cheek with foreigners, although this is changing in cities. Indians demonstrate much respect when meeting or greeting their guests. They will often go out of their way to make you feel extra welcome. They are not known for being punctual but will expect foreigners to be on time. They prefer a formal method of address and will quite happily used the terms "sir" or "madam" rather frequently in conversations. A professional title is expected to be used as in the prefixes Professor, Doctor, Mr., Mrs., or Madam. Business cards are usually exchanged respectfully and the right hand is always used in all transactions. Meetings can be lengthy and time consuming with distractions that can be frustrating. Discussions are almost always led by the most senior person. Refreshments are often served during meetings.

Invitations to the home are very common as hospitality is a deep-rooted value. A small gift may be brought along for the host. The hostess will go out of her way to prepare dishes that you may like. Indians are very sensitive to public criticism as respect and reputation (the equivalent of the Chinese "face") is very important in Indian society. Disagreements are rarely expressed openly and the culture is one of accommodation. Saying "no" is not considered respectful and hence an Indian will go along with your suggestion and proposal though he may not agree with you. One has to be cognizant of this indirect conveyance and learn to interpret non-verbal or other cues to read the situation. Indians are also very compliant and are wont to adhere to policy very closely. Official correspondence may often be very lengthy and wordy with abundant use of flowery and decorative language. Raising issues publicly is not their way and Indians prefer to address concerns and queries after the meeting in a private conversation and often in the company of like-minded colleagues or supporters. Indian English has its own uniqueness both in terms of accent and pronunciation and will need a keen ear to decipher. They also do not feel the need to use common Western terms such as "thank you" or "please" to show appreciation and may respond only with a nod of the head. This does not mean that they are impolite, as their mode of expression of pleasure or gratitude is mostly by non-verbal gestures.

CHAPTER 2

Realizing the Potential: The Markets

As India opens up to the world, it is developing rapidly as a meaningful market for business and investment. At first glance the large population numbers seem remarkably inviting, but closer examination shows that this is misleading, as although India has a large consumer base, the majority of its population is rural and with low income and limited purchasing power. This chapter examines the growing market sectors of India including market segments based on purchasing power, the emerging Indian multinational enterprises (MNEs), the entrenched knowledge and business processing industry, public sector, and state owned enterprises and family owned businesses.

Growth Sectors and Opportunities

Infrastructure

The Indian government has made infrastructure development a priority. It has announced this in its Budget and Economic Survey 2010–2011: "One of the major requirements for sustainable and inclusive economic growth is an extensive and efficient infrastructure network. It is critical for the effective functioning of the economy and industry. The key to global competitiveness of the Indian economy lies in building a high-class infrastructure. To accelerate the pace of infrastructure development and reduce the infrastructure deficit, the government has initiated a host of projects and schemes to upgrade physical infrastructure in all crucial sectors."[1] The ten official infrastructure sectors are: electricity, roads and bridges, ports, airports, telecommunications, railways, irrigation, water supply and sanitation, storage, and oil and gas pipelines.

Investment in infrastructure has averaged 8.37% of the GDP and the contribution of the private sector has been around 34%, higher than the targeted 30%. India has the second largest urban population in the world, amounting to about 285 million and it is expected to constitute 38% of the population by 2026. Rapid urbanization demands improvement in urban infrastructure covering basic civil services like drinking water supply, sewerage, solid-waste management, and urban transport. Municipalities are presently facing acute shortages of capacity and resources. Financing urban investments alone will amount to $1.2 trillion over the coming two decades, averaging $595 per capita, which translates to around 7–8% of the GDP versus the current 0.6%. Funding is to come through a combination of public investment, joint ventures, and exclusive private investment where possible. To stimulate and increase private sector investment from both domestic and foreign sources, 100% foreign direct investment (FDI) is allowed in all infrastructure sectors including roads, power, ports, and airports; 74% in telecom services and 100% in telephone equipment; 49–100% in various services in the aviation sector; extended tax holiday periods to enterprises engaged in the business of development, operation, and maintenance of infrastructure facilities. Emphasis has been placed on joint public and private partnership (PPPs) as a preferred mode for project implementation and the appraisal mechanism for PPP projects has been streamlined to "ensure speed, eliminate delays, adopt international best practices, and have uniformity in appraisal mechanism and guidelines."[2]

Aviation

India is the ninth largest market for aviation in the world. It is the fourth largest in the world in terms of domestic traffic after the United States, China, and Japan. However, India remains one of the least penetrated. Aviation has been a neglected sector for a long time. The civil aviation sector has now been growing rapidly to meet increasing demand and averaging 18% since 2004, with traffic expected to increase to 225–420 million passengers by 2020. In 2010, passengers handled amounted to only 140 million. For a country with a population of over a billion people with a sizeable middle class (200–250 million) the size of the aviation sector is relatively small. Traffic flow is currently located in five major cities exclusively: Mumbai in the west, Delhi in the north, Kolkata in the east, and Chennai and Bangalore in the south. Cargo handled currently is 1.8 million metric tons and is growing at 8% annually. The government has announced its intention to modernize 35 non-metro airports to world-class standards at an estimated cost of $1.2 billion. These include airports at Coimbatore, Tiruchi, Thiruvananthapuram, Visakhapatnam, Port Blair, Mangalore, Agatti, and Pune. Greenfield airports are also approved at Navi Mumbai, Goa, Durgapur, Kannur, and Saras.[3]

In addition to airport development and ground support equipment requirements ($500 million in the next three years), growth in aviation subsectors such as technology-driven communication services has been budgeted at around $100 million for procurement of equipment from abroad. Also growing is the aerospace sector—Hindustan Aeronautics Limited (HAL) was ranked 40th in *Flight International's* top 100 aerospace companies in 2010. An Aerospace and Precision Engineering Special Economic Zone (SEZ) with investment of $641.2 million is to be built in Andhra Pradesh. Boeing is in the process of setting up $100 million maintenance repair overhaul (MRO) facilities in Delhi, and Air India is in the process of launching a Cargo Hub in Nagpur. Deccan Aviation already has one operating there.[4]

Power

Even though India has the fifth largest power generation capacity in the world, the demand for electricity has not kept up with supply and current power supply is at least 30% below demand (2011). The power sector is plagued by capacity shortages, which has resulted in frequent blackouts due to poor infrastructure and reliability as well as redistribution to industry and agriculture from domestic supply. Government and private sector companies generate and supply power in India with the central government owning 33%, state governments 51%, and private companies the remaining 16%. The Indian government has set ambitious goals for the next few years for the power sector, which is poised for significant expansion. To provide availability of over 1,000 units of per capita (from the current 720 units) of electricity by the year 2012, it has been estimated that capacity addition of more than 100,000 megawatts would be required. This has resulted in massive addition plans being proposed in the subsectors of generation, transmission, and distribution.[5]

The government has created an Integrated Energy Policy, which calls for reforms of the power sector to meet energy requirements in the year 2030 that are expected to reach 950,000 megawatts. The aim is to bring about public and private sector collaboration to meet the estimated $1.2 trillion investment required. Rural electrification for approximately 50,000 villages has been sanctioned and remains a priority. The demand for green technologies is also expanding to meet targets of greenhouse gas emission reductions. India is among the top four countries in the world for renewable energy capacity and offers incentives in wind, hydro, biomass, solar, and waste-to-energy projects. It is also seeking to adopt international technology for clean coal infrastructure and is targeting an eight-fold increase from current capacity by 2025.

Telecommunications

India has one of the fastest growing telecommunication sectors in the world with growth of 20% annually. From 2012–2017, it would require investment of $148 billion from private sector operators while the rest would come from state-run telecom companies. Private sector participation in telephone connections increased to 84.5% in 2010 from a meager 5% in 1999. Urban and rural teledensity (telecom penetration) rose from 7.02% in 2004 to 64.34% in 2010. Private sector contribution to rural telephone growth reached 84.5% in 2010. Cellular subscriber base is 827 million currently (2011) and expected to reach 1.2 billion by 2017. To meet this demand, operators will have to invest $31 billion on 2G networks and $34 billion on 3G or 4G equipment, $9 billion on transmission equipment and about $23 billion on passive infrastructure. In addition, the government expects to spend $23 billion on purchasing spectrum through auction and $11 billion on consumer premise equipment.[6]

Demand for broadband wireless access (BWA) is also growing rapidly. It is expected to reach 11 million by 2013 from the current 1.25 million, an increase of 144% per annum. 3G subscribers are growing at a rate of 82% per year and will reach 22 million by 2013. Mobile

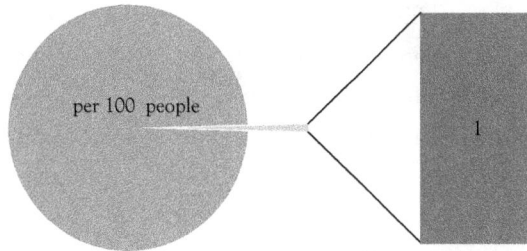

(A) Fixed broadband internet subscribers

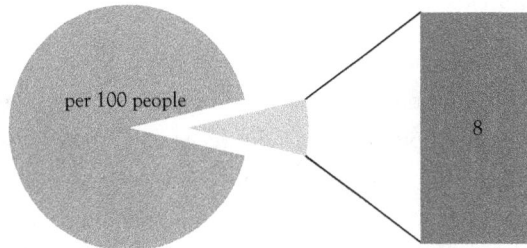

(B) Internet users

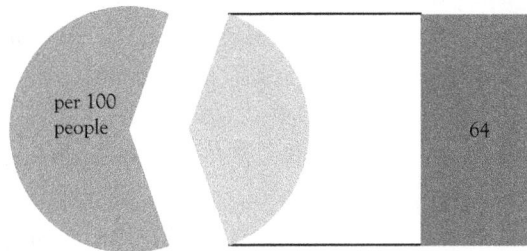

(C) Cellular phones subscribers

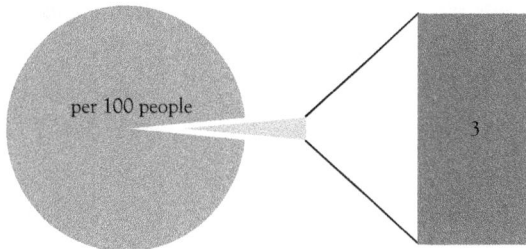

(D) Telephone lines subscribers

Figure 2.1. Telecommunication infrastructure.

Source: Adapted from Index Mundi 2010 (data compiled from Index Mundi 2010). Retrieved February 25, 2012, from http://www.indexmundi.com/facts/india#Infrastructure

number portability (MNP) was launched in 2010 and will this year reach 700 million subscribers across the country. The rising demand for wire-line telecom equipment and wireless core equipment using state-of-the-art technology is opening the door for manufacturing in India. Several well-known telecom companies have already set up operations and begun to export telecom equipment due to the incentives offered, low labor costs, and large talent pool for research and development (R&D).

Oil and Gas

India's energy needs, especially in oil and gas, are expected to increase rapidly in the coming years. Oil and gas constitute around 45% of total energy consumption. India imports around 80% of its oil needs but in recent years it has emerged as one of the regions with the most prospective oil and gas discoveries onshore and offshore. Since 1999, the government has awarded 47.3% of its sedimentary basin for exploration. So far 87 oil and gas discoveries have been made by private and joint venture companies. In 2010 alone, 34 exploration blocks including 8 deep-water, 7 shallow-water, and 19 on-land blocks under the New Exploration Licensing Policy (NELP) were offered.

India's sedimentary basins are still relatively underexplored. The government is thus planning to replace the NELP with a new policy, the Open Acreage Licensing Policy (OALP). Under this policy, companies can choose any block for offer at any time, without waiting for the regular bid rounds under NELP. The blocks will be awarded to the party giving the best bid at any time of the year. India has also revised the production-sharing contract and streamlined the bidding and review process. The Indian government is seeking investments in excess of $100 billion for the next 15 years in both the upstream and downstream sectors. Petroleum products consumption has been growing by at least 5% annually and demand is expected to reach 368 metric tons per year by 2025.[7]

Food Processing

India is among the largest producers and consumers of food products, especially since it is largely a dairy-based and vegetarian nation. Total market size is around $92 billion. Each individual in India spends about

30% of his income on food. The huge customer base has experienced an increase of about 8% in disposable income over the last five years. This, in turn, has led to a 20% increase in per capita food expenditure. Besides, between 2005 and 2015, a 300% growth of the middle to rich class and an 11% growth in youth population (15–25 years) are expected.

However, the food industry in India is still developing. Food processing is still lagging behind; only 2% of fruits and vegetables and about 15% of milk are processed. In spite of this, the industry ranks 5th in size and represents 6.3% of GDP. It also accounts for 13% of exports and 6% of total industrial investment. The food processing industry is estimated at $70 billion, which includes $22 billion of value-added products. India produces 600 million tons of food grains per year. It ranks first in the world in production of cereals and milk. It is the second largest exporter of rice, fifth largest exporter of wheat in the world, and its agriculture exports account for 12% of total exports. It is the second largest producer of fruits and vegetables and ranks in the top five producers of groundnuts, tea, coffee, spices, sugar, and oilseeds. India is also the seventh largest producer of fish and stands second in the world in aquaculture. The country is poised for agricultural diversification as well as growth in food processing. Food production is expected to double by 2020. Food processing technology, equipment, skills, and services are expected to attract $33 billion in investment in 10 years. The government is creating agricultural zones and mega food parks in various cities to attract FDI. Food processing has been declared a priority sector.

Manufacturing

India is ranked second in the world in terms of manufacturing capability, according to the "2010 Global Manufacturing Competitiveness Index" by Deloitte Touche Tohmatsu and the US Council on Competitiveness.[8] Net contribution of the manufacturing sector to GDP is in excess of 25% and growth averaged around 8–9% in the past decade, with a slowdown in 2010. It is expected to grow in excess of 10% in the coming decade due to continued increase in demand. The manufacturing sector is estimated to command a market capitalization of $520 billion by 2014–2015. This sector is very wide and covers all kinds of manufacturing activities including automobiles and auto parts, textiles and garments, steel and other metal products, chemicals and chemical products, gems and jewelry, electronics hardware, machinery and machine tools, light and heavy engineering, mining and mineral processing equipment, leather and leather products, rubber and plastics, paper products, and consumer durable and non-durable goods.

Machinery and equipment is a growth area in the manufacturing sector. It is expected to reach an output of $682 billion by end 2011 and a turnover of $851 million by end 2012. It anticipates investment of $880 million over the next 10 years in technology development for automotive, aerospace, defense, healthcare, and energy machine tools.[9] The Indian machine tools industry is ranked 8th in terms of global consumption but is only 19th in terms of machine tools manufacturing.

Another growth area is in *mining and mineral processing equipment*. India is endowed with many mineral resources. It produces 87 minerals and has approximately 2,500 operational mines. The industry employs over a million people and produces mica, barites, coal and lignite, iron ore, chromite, bauxite, and manganese. Growth averages 12% per annum. India is ranked 3rd in the world in coal production. It plans to invest $30–40 billion in the coming decade in developing new coalmines. India will need state-of-the-art equipment and machinery. The government has been encouraging FDI inflow by gradually fine-tuning and liberalizing regulations to allow up to 100% FDI via the automatic route. Privatization of mines is also taking place at a rapid rate. The Indian market for mining and mineral equipment is estimated at over $2 billion.[10]

The *textile industry* is another fast growing area with growth of about 11% a year and expected to reach $15 billion by 2012. The government is taking action to encourage investments, increase markets, upgrade quality, encourage global participation, and adopt world-class practices, standards, and technology. India is becoming a hub for technical textiles in sectors such as automobiles, electronics, and telecommunications, food processing, packing, and healthcare. Market opportunities exist in both the production and trading of products for domestic consumption as well as exports. Some products that use technical textiles are: diapers, polypropylene spun bound fabric for disposables, wipes, protective clothing, hoses, and webbing for seat belts. Packaging technology leads the segment and is expected to grow by 13% by 2012–2013.

Services

The contribution of India's services sector to its economy is a whopping 55.2% of the GDP and is growing 10% annually, contributing to about a quarter of total employment, accounting for a high share in FDI inflows and over one third of total exports.[11] The subsectors are: domestic trade, financing and insurance, tourism including hotels and restaurants, shipping and port services, storage, telecommunications related services, real estate, information technology (IT) and IT-enabled services (ITeS), accounting and auditing services, research and development (R&D) services, legal services and consultancy, and specialized services such as sports. The two fast-growing broad services categories are first, finance, insurance, real estate, and business services; and second, transport, storage, and communication. Annual growth rate in India's services GDP at factor cost in constant prices for the 2005–10 period averaged 8% in trade, hotels, and restaurants; 13% in transport, storage, and communications; 12.5% in financing, insurance, real estate, and business services; and 10% in community, social, and personal services.

The *IT and BPO industry* is poised to become a $225 billion industry by 2020 and has become one of the most significant growth catalysts for the Indian economy. The sector is estimated to have grown by 19% in 2011, clocking revenue of almost $76 billion. India's outsourcing industry has witnessed a rebound and registered better than expected growth. Export revenues are estimated to have totaled $59 billion in 2011 and contributed to 26% of total Indian exports. The workforce in the IT industry will touch 30 million by 2020 and this sunrise industry is expected to continue its growth pattern. The country's domestic market for BPO is projected to grow over 23% to touch $1.4 billion in 2011, $1.69 billion in 2012, and $2.47 billion by 2014. The Indian IT sector continues to be one of the sunshine sectors of the Indian economy showing rapid growth and promise. The exports component of this industry is expected to reach $175 billion in revenue by 2020. The domestic component will contribute $50 billion in revenue by 2020. Together, the export and domestic markets are likely to bring in $225 billion in revenue, as new opportunities emerge in areas such as the public and healthcare sectors, as well as when countries like Brazil, Russia, China, and Japan opt for greater outsourcing.[12]

The **tourism industry** in India is still underdeveloped in comparison with those of other emerging economies. Still, the Indian tourism and hospitality industry is the largest service sector in the country, which adds around 6.23% to the national GDP and 8.78% of the total employment in the country. It also plays an important role in the country's foreign exchange earnings, as its share in India's export earnings accounted for 13% of the total export services in 2010. India's tourism industry is experiencing a strong period of growth, driven by the burgeoning Indian middle class, growth in high spending foreign tourists, and coordinated government campaigns to promote "Incredible India." The country is fast becoming a major global destination. India's travel and tourism industry is also one of the most profitable industries in the country. Tourist arrivals have been increasing annually to around 6 million in 2011. The hotel and restaurants sector is an important subcomponent of the tourism sector. Presently there are 1,593 classified hotels with a capacity of 95,000 rooms in the country. Studies have indicated a demand–supply gap of 150,000 hotel rooms, of which 100,000 rooms are in the budget segment.[13] Various financial and fiscal incentives have been announced by the government including tax holidays, relaxation of external commercial borrowing limits, allowing FDI up to 100% for the hotel and tourism-related industry, and delinking of credit to hotel projects from commercial real estate. High-end international hoteliers including Four Seasons Hotels & Resorts, Shangri-La Hotels & Resorts, Fairmont Hotels & Resorts, Park Hyatt Hotels, J.W. Marriott, and Relais & Chateaux plan to significantly expand their presence in India in the next several years.[14]

The **construction industry** in India contributed around 8% to the national GDP in 2011 with anticipated growth rate of 8.6% per annum between 2011 and 2016. It is an important indicator of national development through infrastructure, residential, and commercial projects. The industry is rather fragmented with a handful of major companies involved in construction activities across all segments; medium-sized companies specializing in niche activities; and small and medium contractors who actually work on a subcontract basis. The sector is highly labor-intensive, providing employment to more than 35 million people. There are many initiatives by the government to undertake projects on PPP basis. These initiatives have resulted in more private ownership of build–operate–transfer (BOT), build–operate–own–transfer (BOOT), and build–operate–lease–transfer (BOLT) projects. FDI is allowed up to 100% under the automatic route in townships, housing, built-up infrastructure, and construction of development projects (which include housing, commercial premises, educational institutions, and recreational facilities).

India's large *retail sector* is the fifth largest in the world (after the United States, China, the United Kingdom, and Germany) and is valued in excess of $500 billion in 2011. However, the organized part constitutes only around 5–7% and has huge potential for growth, which remains largely untapped. The organized sector is projected to be worth $280 billion by 2017 with total retail in excess of $1 trillion. The demand will need establishment of logistics and supply chain infrastructure as well as new and advanced retail technologies. The large rural market is also full of opportunities for domestic and global players. Hypermarkets are slowly gaining prominence, a refocus from the burgeoning supermarkets and small formats of several years ago. Food accounts for 70% of Indian retail, but it remains under-penetrated by organized retail. Organized retail has a 31% share in clothing and apparel and continues to see growth in this sector. The home segment shows promise, growing 20–30% per year. Food retail growth is of great significance and opportunity for both domestic and international corporations. Early entrants have already gained a meaningful hold. The government's decision to open the multibrand retail sector to foreign retailers (51% equity in Indian operations) in November 2011 met with a major outcry from domestic firms as well as opposition politicians, though it was supported by the Retailers Association of India. Though this is a major setback, it is only a matter of time until this reform is implemented and multinational retailers like Wal-Mart, Tesco, Carrefour, and IKEA become major participants.

The Indian *financial services* sector has been slow in opening up for investment but has huge potential. The insurance industry has undergone several changes in trends and policies in the year 2010. The $41 billion industry is considered the fifth largest life insurance market, and is growing at a rapid pace of 32–34% annually, according to the Life Insurance Council. FDI up to 26% in the insurance sector is allowed under the automatic route. The banking industry has traditionally been one of the most regulated industries in India. However, with opening up of the economy in most sectors, this industry has been no exception and has experienced a gradual phased deregulation. The limit for FDI in private banks has been increased from 49% to 74% and the 10% cap on voting rights has been removed. In addition, the limit for foreign institutional investment in private banks is 49%. Indian banks are also looking to expand in locations out of India in a big way.

Healthcare

The Indian healthcare industry is growing exponentially due to the growth in population (1.6% per year), higher expectations due to better education, affluence and rise of a large middle class, greater availability of health insurance and medical infrastructure, and increasing demand from medical tourism. The healthcare sector is poised to touch $280 billion by the year 2020, thereby contributing to 7–8% of GDP by 2012. A $36 billion industry today and growing at 15% compound annual growth rate, the healthcare industry will reach a market value of $280 billion by 2022.[15] Medical infrastructure is still poorly developed in India (especially in rural areas) and unable to meet the rising demand for quality service. An additional 1 million beds are needed by 2012 to bring the bed-to-thousand population ratio to 1.85. Private sector investment in healthcare has been increasing faster than government investment to meet the average 15% growth in medical infrastructure. Hundred percent FDI is permitted for health and medical services under the automatic route. Specialty and super-specialty hospital facilities, upgrading of present hospital facilities, and high-end medical equipment and medical consumables are needed. Opportunities also exist in the area of hospital management, provision of health insurance, and manufacture of medical equipment in India.

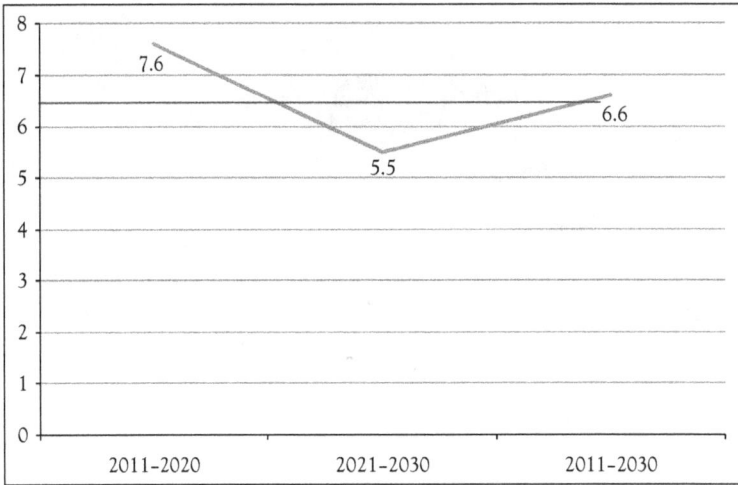

Figure 2.2. GDP forecast.

Source: Adapted from Business without Borders. Country Briefing 2011b (data compiled from Global Opportunity Tool). Retrieved February 25, 2012, from http://country.eiu.com/article.aspx?articleid=1038359288&Country=India& topic=Economy&subtopic=Long-term+outlook&subsubtopic=India-highlights%3a+Long-term+outlook

Emerging Regions, States, and Cities

Development in India has been traditionally lopsided. Severe imbalances exist in regional infrastructure availability. Inter-state disparities include politics, economy, education, culture, language, social stratification, poverty, industry, market size, income, output, technology, and pro-business government. While some cities and states are relatively prosperous and modern, others are seriously underdeveloped with significant poverty. The following is a useful description of India's four main geographic regions:[16]

The **western** region of India is a relatively prosperous region of the country. The state of Maharashtra has Mumbai, the world's third most populous city and India's business and entertainment capital. It is among India's most urbanized states, with some 42% of its people living in cities, more than half of these in slums. Despite an abundance of urban poor, the state ranks relatively high in measures of health, education, and infrastructure, and Mumbai itself has some of the world's highest real estate prices. Further to the west, the state of Gujarat has a particularly productive agricultural sector and is the region's most lucrative investment environment,

Major cities in India

with social and infrastructure measures nearing those of Maharashtra. Other western states of Rajasthan and Madhya Pradesh rank in the middle range on such measures. In the southwest, the small state of Goa - a former Portuguese colony - has the country's highest per capita income.

In the **north** is Delhi, India's national capital. It is also the most affluent of India's administrative districts with a per capita income double the national average. Along with Delhi, the medium-sized northern states of Punjab, Himachal Pradesh, and Haryana form India's most prosperous region, as well as its largest market for many products and services. However, immediately to the east, Uttar Pradesh is the most populous and among the poorest of Indian states, consistently ranking low on development indicators. Further to the north and isolated by mountainous terrain is the state of Jammu and Kashmir, which has been suffering the effects of a religion-based insurgency since 1989. Still, this state has relatively low poverty rates.

The *south* is where recent global attention on India has focused. Its fast-growing states of Karnataka and Andhra Pradesh have been at the forefront of the country's widely touted software and IT boom (along with Delhi). Their respective capital cities - Bangalore and Hyderabad - have earned fame as emerging hubs for high-technology research and services, as well as for BPO centers which serve many of the world's largest corporations. Other southern states are Kerala, known for its excellent social infrastructure and a 91% literacy rate, and Tamil Nadu, with its major commercial and industrial capital of Chennai (formerly Madras), said by some to be India's best-governed state. Despite the massive infrastructural and environmental problems caused by the rapid growth of its cities, India's southern region has been dubbed the country's most livable.

The numerous states of India's *east and northeast* face historical and geographical disadvantages that include inaccessibility and several ongoing armed insurgencies. This region thus continues to be India's least developed and its infrastructure remains quite poor. Bihar, India's poorest state, Orissa, Jharkhand, and Chhattisgarh rank at the bottom of most development indices. West Bengal, with the megacity and former British colonial capital of Calcutta (now officially called Kolkata) is eastern India's fastest-growing and most important commercial, industrial, and agricultural (jute) center. For long a stronghold of India's communist parties, West Bengal has this year (2011) seen a change in direction. The "Seven Sisters" - smaller northeastern states connected to the rest of India by a 20-mile-wide "Chicken Neck" - are relatively sparsely populated and are distinguished by considerable religious and ethnic diversity. One result has been armed tribal and separatist conflicts, some of which pre-date Indian independence, that present major obstacles to economic development.

There are many opportunities in cities beyond the metros of Mumbai and New Delhi. Tier II and III cities in India are growing at an even faster rate than the metros. They are less competitive, less costly, and frequently more "business friendly" with full wireless and broadband connectivity.

Their young, educated, and increasingly ambitious workforces have both aspirations and spending power. While Mumbai and New Delhi continue to be the biggest contributing hubs to India's economy, emerging cities are outperforming the metros in terms of GDP growth. The Tier II cities hold the key to India's future growth and offer many profitable opportunities to overseas businesses. Companies in the emerging cities are quickly developing an appetite for know-how, infrastructure, and venture capital, seeking to capture the benefits of India's economic development. Many Indian companies are open to the prospects of international partnerships and are often highly diversified. Studies have found Bangalore, Chennai, Hyderabad, Kolkata, and Pune to be suitable for business success.[17]

Bangalore is the capital of the state of Karnataka. It is located in the southeastern part of the state and is considered the fourth largest GDP contributor in the country. Bangalore enjoys a temperate climate year-round. The city is one of the most diverse and multicultural in India, having gone through a major transformation with the influx of migrants from other Indian states and a ten-fold growth in the last decade. Today, the city is home to over 10,000 "dollar-millionaires," leading to a vast concentration of wealth. The city is well connected, thanks to the newly built Bengaluru International Airport, and is well suited for hosting world-class conferences and exhibitions. It is known as the Silicon Valley of India with the state's IT and ITeS exports valued at $16.3 billion in 2008–2009. Bangalore is known for its high level of literacy and education and has a large concentration of scientific research institutions and development centers. The tertiary sector contributes more than half of the state's income. Large businesses like Infosys and Wipro are based here. Communications is one of the fastest growing sectors, reporting a 26% growth rate in 2008–2009, while advertising is generating scores of new jobs in the city. Other fast-growing sectors in Bangalore include communications, banking and insurance, and business services.

Chennai is India's fourth largest metropolitan city and the fifth largest economic hub based on GDP. Formerly known as Madras, Chennai is the capital of the state of Tamil Nadu and is a major center for music, art, and culture. Close to many cultural and natural attractions, tourism is one of its priority economic sectors with a growth rate of 11.9% in trade, hotels, and restaurants. Chennai is known as the "Gateway to South India" and has a highly skilled, English speaking workforce. Chennai's international airport has recently expanded its air cargo import complex and the city's port is one of the state's major seaports handling mainly container cargo. To counter traffic congestion, Chennai has a well-established suburban railway network, an elevated mass rapid transit system and plans for a metro rail project. Chennai's standard of education is highly rated in the country and higher education is strong in areas such as engineering and medicine. The city's economy is supported by industries such as automotive, technology, healthcare, IT and ITeS, financial services, retail, and textiles. Tamil Nadu has attracted significant FDI in recent years and government incentives have included a strong promotion of industrial clusters and Special Economic Zones (SEZs). In Chennai, SEZs are mostly dedicated to IT and ITeS, apparel, and automobiles. Chennai is known worldwide as a strong exporter of woven garments and a hub for automotive manufacturing and exports. The Tamil film industry contributes significantly to the state's economy, with Chennai standing at the forefront of Tamil filmmaking. Major Indian and foreign financial institutions have a presence with banks like ABN AMRO and the World Bank sustaining back office operations in the city.

Hyderabad, the state capital of Andhra Pradesh, is famous for its rich history and culture. Also famous for its leading position as producer of precious and semi-precious gems and pearls, Hyderabad is known as the "city of pearls." Hyderabad typically has tropical weather with a hot, dry season and a wet monsoon season. The Hyderabad international airport is well connected to cities like Amsterdam, London, Chicago, Frankfurt, Kuala Lumpur, Singapore, Dubai, and major Indian destinations. The city has actively promoted itself as a prime destination for international conferences and offers state-of-the-art hotels and convention centers. There are also plans to build an elevated mass rapid transit system. The state of Andhra Pradesh has set an ambitious economic plan, targeting a 9% annual growth by 2012–2013. The city's economy has traditionally been dominated by the service industry; however, in recent years Hyderabad has diversified into other sectors such as trade, commerce, communication, IT, and ITeS. Pharmaceuticals and biotechnology have also become a strong economic sector, with half of the top 10 pharmaceutical companies in the country based in Hyderabad, along with a number of research institutes. The emergence of IT in Hyderabad is already earning it the title of India's next Silicon Valley. The government offers a number of fiscal and sector policy incentives, which include SEZs and industrial clusters to attract even further FDI. Clusters in Hyderabad are typically in the IT and ITeS sectors, pharmaceuticals and biotech, and textiles and apparel. The state's share of IT exports has risen steadily, supported by 14 operational IT/ITeS SEZs in the state. It is home to Microsoft's India Development Centre, which employs approximately 1,500 personnel. The city is also emerging as a prominent gaming and animation hub, with local companies catering mainly for outsourced work for film, commercial, and games production houses in North America and Europe. Hyderabad is home to many animation, multimedia, recording, film, and post-production studios. Two of India's most renowned universities are based in Hyderabad and they offer degrees in business, technology, legal studies, and life sciences, making Hyderabad an important center for learning that attracts students from all over India and overseas (Africa and the Middle East).

Kolkata is the capital of the state of West Bengal. The former capital of India, it has long been considered a cultural center thanks to its literary and artistic tradition. Kolkata is India's third largest urban agglomeration and the third largest contributor to the country's GDP. The state's main industries include IT, apparel, tea, mineral resources, iron, steel, and biotechnology. Kolkata has a tropical wet and dry climate. It is the commercial gateway to eastern India and Southeast Asia with links to Nepal, Bhutan, and China. Kolkata has both an international airport and a major modern port. The "golden quadrilateral," a highway network connecting India's major cities, had been nearly completed between Kolkata and New Delhi, and Kolkata and Chennai as of April 2011. Kolkata is the main financial hub of eastern India, having attracted FDI inflows for $1.3 billion (Kolkata region) during 2000–2009, according to the Department of Industrial Policy and Promotion. The city also offers lower costs of operation compared with other cities. Kolkata's workforce is highly talented and English is largely used as the language of business. There are 18 universities in the state of West Bengal. Kolkata's infrastructure and suitable agro-climatic conditions also support a prominent tea industry with an important presence of tea producers, traders, and exporters based in the city. West Bengal is a state with abundant mineral resources. Its iron ore deposits make it a favored destination for the steel industry. SEZs in Kolkata mainly operate in garments, engineering, IT/ITeS, and biotechnology.

Pune is the second largest city in the state of Maharashtra and is located 150 km east of Mumbai, the state's capital. Pune is a renowned tourist destination, home to many historical monuments, palaces, and museums. Maharashtra is planning a 1,000 MW power plant to exclusively meet Pune's growing electricity demands. The Mumbai–Pune expressway, a 93 km six-lane highway, connects the two cities with a journey of approximately two hours. Pune's Lohegaon Airport operates international flights. Pune is a strong player in the engineering and automotive industries, food and agro, and IT/ITeS. Pune has a tropical wet and dry climate. This city has boomed in recent years thanks to the establishment of several SEZs and industrial clusters in IT/ITeS, hardware and software, electronics, pharmaceuticals and biotech, and food and agro. Companies like Frito Lay and Coca Cola are located in Pune. The city has received considerable investment for the development of its urban infrastructure. Pune is an important education hub, with its schools and colleges known for their quality of education. Some of the most popular educational institutions are Symbiosis International University, Pune University, Bharati Vidyapeeth, Institute of Armament Technology, and Dr. D.Y. Patil University. The state of Maharashtra accounts for 38% of the country's automobile manufacturing and Pune is one of its major production centers. The engineering sector in Pune is highly diversified with an important output of engineering goods, machinery, and automotive parts. Pune's IT and electronics sector has grown considerably, largely due to the many industrial clusters and SEZs dotted around the city. Major software companies have operating and BPO centers, back-end support services, R&D, and captive facilities in Pune. The city's retail sector is expected to witness a 51% compounded growth over the next five years, one of the most active markets in western India.

A study "Economic Freedom of the States of India, 2011" co-published by the Cato Institute[18] rated the various states according to *size of government, legal structure and security of property rights, and regulation of business and labor.* The main highlights of this study (2009) are as follows (Figure 2.3):

- The top three states in economic freedom in 2009 were Tamil Nadu, Gujarat, and Andhra Pradesh, in that order
- The bottom three states in 2009, in reverse order, were Bihar, Uttarakhand, and Assam
- The state with the fastest improvement in economic freedom was Andhra Pradesh
- The second fastest improving state was Gujarat
- Even as some states improved in economic freedom, others worsened, showing that there is no uniform all-India trend
- Only two states registered large increases in economic freedom: Andhra Pradesh and Gujarat. Haryana, Tamil Nadu, West Bengal, Rajasthan and Jammu & Kashmir registered moderate increases in economic freedom

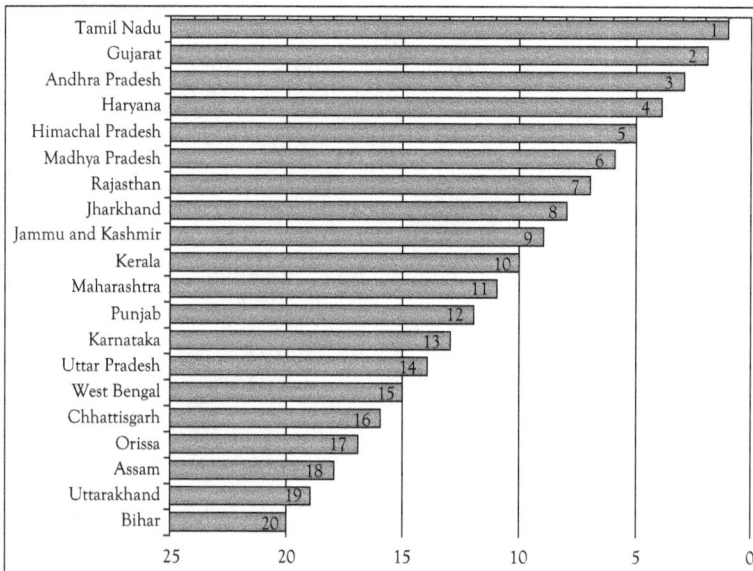

Figure 2.3. Ranking of Indian states on economic freedom.

Source: Adapted from The Indian School of Business (ISB) and the Vale Columbia Center on Sustainable International Investment (VCC). The growth story of Indian multinationals. Retrieved September 28, 2011, from http://www.vcc.columbia.edu/files/vale/documents/India_2009.pdf

- The states with the largest decreases in economic freedom were Madhya Pradesh, Orissa, Uttarakhand, Punjab, and Himachal Pradesh
- Punjab, once among the best performers, slipped from 6th position in 2005 to 12th position in 2009. It has been riding too long on its earlier successes, and its present track record on governance, broadly defined, is anything but satisfactory

Doing business is easier in Ludhiana, Hyderabad, and Bhubaneshwar. It is more difficult to start and operate a business in Kochi and Kolkata. The World Bank report "Doing Business in India, 2011" has ranked Indian cities according to the ease in starting a business, dealing with construction permits, registering property, paying taxes, trading across borders, enforcing contracts, and resolving insolvency.[19] Its findings are illustrated in Fig. 2.4.

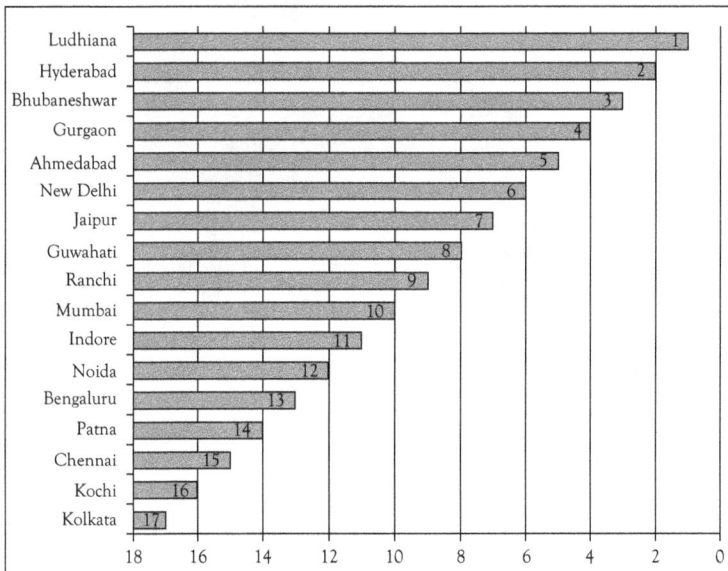

Figure 2.4. Easiest cities for doing business in India.

Source: Adapted from The World Bank Group. Doing Business in India 2009. Retrieved January 7, 2012, from http://www.doingbusiness.org/rankings/India/

Market Segments: Upper, Middle, and Lower Pyramids

India's population of 1.2 billion of various income groups and diversities provides manufacturers, entrepreneurs, enterprises, educationists, NGOs, and philanthropists with enormous opportunities to fulfill varied economic and social needs of different classes of consumers.

India's population is young. Twenty-nine percent of this population is below the age of 14 years and only 5% is above 65 years of age. Hence the majority of the wage-earning population of 63% belongs to the "target consumers" group, which represents 756 million people. This stratum can be further classified into the upper-income group, middle-income group, and the lower-income group (Figure 2.5).[20]

Upper-Income Group: This affluent group is categorized as *Global India*. This group has an average annual household income of over $19,000. In 2005, it represented 1% of the total population of 1.1 billion.[21] Members of this group own assets, and consume luxury products and services such as branded jewelry, apparel, electronic gadgets and devices, and automobiles. They vacation abroad and have

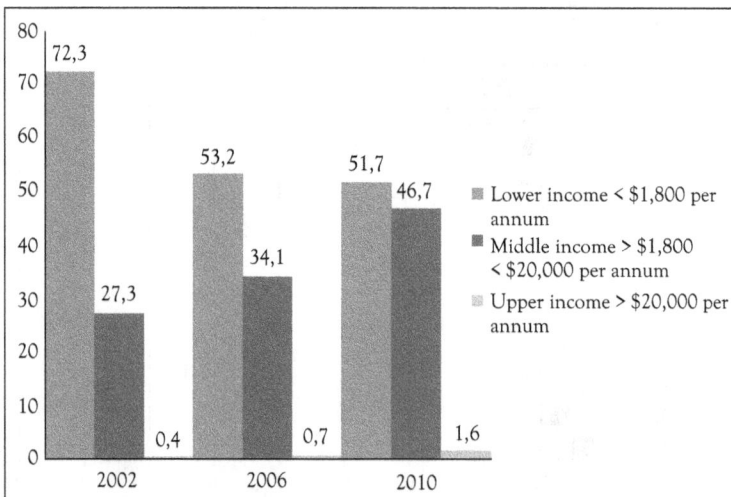

Figure 2.5. Income segments (%).

Source: Adapted from NCAER, Alchemy Research. Retrieved January 7, 2012, from http://maple-advisors.com/Maple%20Capital%20Advisors%20-%20India%20Consumer%20Story.pdf

a lifestyle similar to their counterparts in the developed countries.[22] In 2010, the luxury market saw robust growth of 20%, reaching $5.75 billion. However, the fastest growth lies in the luxury products market at 29%, which is over and above the growth rate in the luxury market segment as well as above the expectations of 23%.[23]

"The luxury industry in India has shown very promising growth over the last couple of years and is set to grow at a minimum of 25% per year over the next few years with India emerging as a luxury shopping destination," said Sanjay Kapoor, Chairman of CII Luxury Goods Forum. It is no wonder, as India has more rich households than most European nations, surpassing Germany and France. It is among the top five countries, after the UAE, Singapore, Hong Kong, and Sweden, where the affluent have more than $1 million to invest on average.[24] There are 55 billionaires whose aggregate wealth of $250 billion is equivalent to almost a sixth of the nation's annual economic output.[25]

Based on the projected population growth rate for 2015 and 2025, the share of population in the upper-income group will increase by 1% if India continues to grow at the current real GDP growth rate of 6–9% annually.[26]

Middle-Income Group: The terminology of the "Great Indian Middle class" was coined by economists and planners in the 1990s.[27] The National Council of Applied Economic Research's (NCAER) definition of the middle class too has evolved over a two-decade period. Apart from using disposable income as the primary criterion to estimate the size of the middle class, cultural parameters such as education, consumption trends, and ownership of select consumer goods is considered to understand the concept of the middle class, which is far from being a homogenous group. The size of the middle class has registered a six-fold increase, from a mere 26 million in 1995–1996 to an estimated 153 million by end 2010 (Figure 2.6).[28] It is also estimated that the middle class will include 41% of the population by 2025, if India maintains its annual 6–9% growth rate.[29] This is a 35% increase from a decade ago, when the middle class included just 6% of the population.

The middle class comprises two economic segments - seekers with real annual household disposable incomes of $3,800–9,500 and strivers at $9,500–19,000. As there is no official definition of the middle class, this group is estimated to range between 30 million and 300 million.

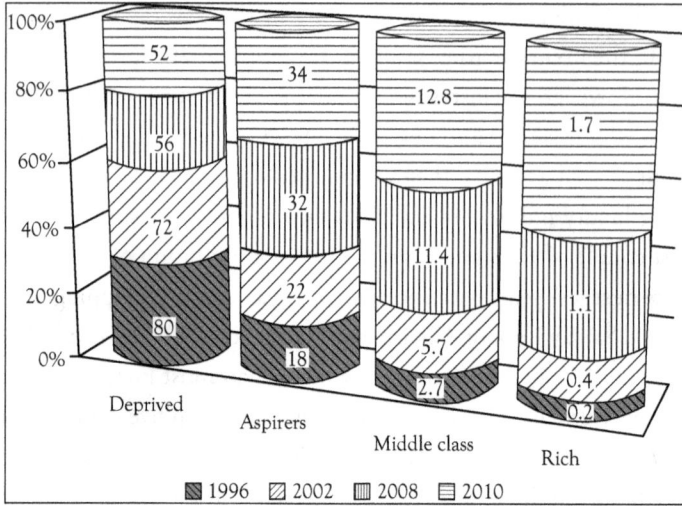

Figure 2.6. Change in income segments (%).

Source: Adapted from NCAER, Alchemy Research. Retrieved January 7, 2012, from http://maple-advisors.com/Maple%20Capital%20Advisors%20-%20India%20Consumer%20Story.pdf

At a conservative level, it represents less than 30% of India's total population. The consumption level is comparable with Ireland's total private consumption and is forecast to triple as a share of India's total consumption over the next 15 years.[30]

Since India started its economic reforms in the 1990s, many foreign enterprises have seized opportunities to tap into the size of the growing middle class only to realize later that their sales figures did not increase exponentially as expected in their calculations. This led to a logical debate of whether the middle class truly had the propensity to spend. The complexities of the middle class are attributable to its different disposable income levels, which eventually dictate their spending behavior. There are three layers. The bottom layer consists of the "Aspirers," who moved up a notch from the bottom of the pyramid (Deprived). The "Aspirers" are the greatest spenders and together with the "Deprived" control 75% of spending, mostly on basic needs. The middle layer consists of the "Seekers," who have surpassed the basic needs stage, and have engaged themselves in activities that represent a good life such as buying new color

TVs, motorcycles, and small cars, eating out in western food outlets, etc. The "Strivers" have the highest disposable income and spend less on basic food necessities and more on consumer durables such as bigger apartments and automobiles.[31]

The distinguishing behavior of the middle class is the demand for equal power. Its members no longer accept high power-distance dealings between themselves, their superiors, and government authority. The middle class is projected to grow at a pace higher than "Global India" and "Destitute India" and hence its size has significant impact on economic, political, and business policies, which in turn affects the aggregate growth of the economy. There is no doubt that the engine of growth in India is the middle class.

The implication of the rise of the middle class by year 2025 with the incremental rise in population size makes it necessary to undertake measures to ensure that the economy is ready and able to accommodate the growing needs and demands of education, healthcare, land and sea transportation, infrastructure, and IT.

Lower-Income Group: The poorest socioeconomic group known as the bottom of the pyramid (BOP) is also the largest. This phase was first used by U.S. President Franklin D. Roosevelt on April 7, 1932 in his radio address[32] and later further extrapolated by Prahalad and Stuart. They argued against the conventional notion that the poor are too economically deficient to respond to the goods and services designed by Multi National Corporations (MNCs) to yield a profitable return of investment. On the contrary, the 4 billion people in the world who are at the bottom of the pyramid do represent a multitrillion-dollar market. This was proven through the success of pioneers such as Nirma, a local company in India, which in the early 1990s, succeeded in penetrating the bottom of the pyramid market in the detergent product segment and generated sustainable profits and fierce competition to cause hindustan lever ltd (HLL) to respond.[33]

In 2009–2010, it was estimated that 51.5% of India's households made up the "Deprived," who earned an annual household income of less than $2,280. The share is much higher in the rural area, which comprises 63% as opposed to only 27% in the urban areas (Figures 2.7 and 2.8).[34] They are mainly illiterate and the majority live in densely populated rural areas with poor living conditions and very poor access to clean water.

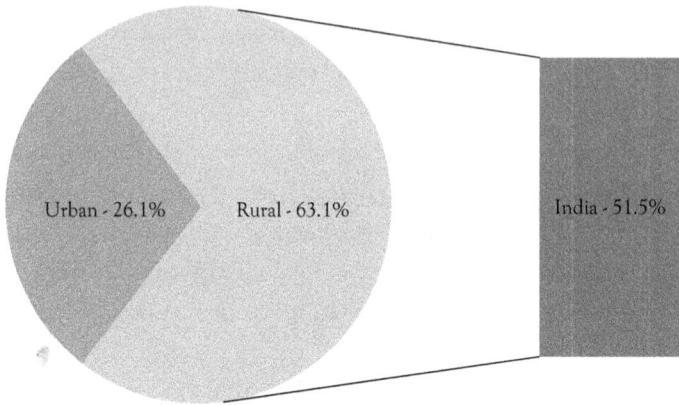

Figure 2.7. Percentage share of household income of the deprived segment by urban and rural area

Source: Adapted from NCAER, Alchemy Research. Retrieved January 7, 2012, from http:// maple- advisors.com/Maple%20Capital%20Advisors%20-%20India%20Consumer%20Story.pdf

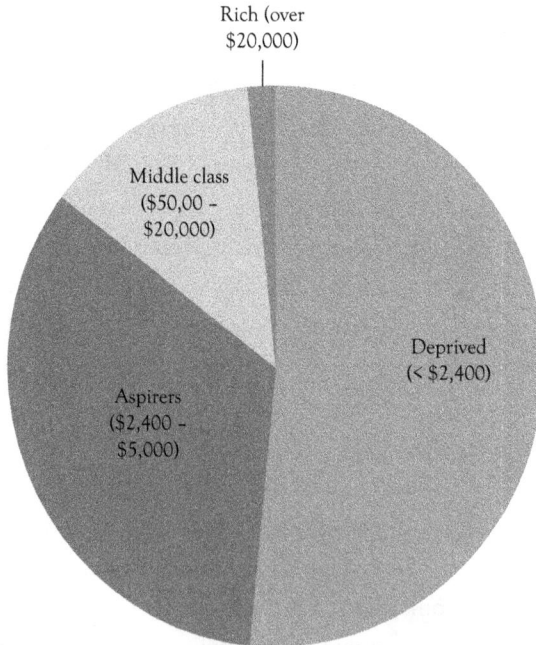

Figure 2.8. India's household income by segments, 2010.

Source: Adapted from NCAER, Alchemy Research. Retrieved January 7, 2012, from http:// maple- advisors.com/Maple%20Capital%20Advisors%20-%20India%20Consumer%20Story.pdf

In addition, they do not have access to financial resources. Their meager wages go toward sustaining the daily food expenditure of the entire household.[35]

The state-run National Commission for Enterprises in the Unorganized Sector (NCEUS) reported that 77% of Indians or 836 million people lived on less than 20 rupees (approximately $0.50 nominal; US$2 PPP) per day.[36] Prahalad and Stuart's argument might hold true in the current situation where the rich stop buying due to the economic downturn. Businesses are already looking into the huge consumer base that lies in the rural market, which still constitutes two thirds of the country's population and about 60% of its GDP. Microfinance companies are also benefiting from the business shift and are able to provide credit to the poor due to the demand for basic housing and electricity needs.[37]

It is clear that the impoverished state of the bottom of the pyramid has an impact on the overall economic performance of the country. Hence their wellbeing can no longer be ignored. The government of India has committed a $5.1 billion fund towards the National Rural Livelihoods Mission (NRLM) to eradicate poverty and improve the livelihood of poor rural people and develop the rural economy. This project is supported by the World Bank with a credit of $1 billion and aims to help the poor create their own savings and assets. It also aims at empowering women, farmers, milk producers, and weavers in rural areas by linking them up with markets and to negotiate better terms of trade for their products and services. The most important program is to provide rural youth with skills and opportunities to secure jobs in India's mainstream economy.[38] According to a McKinsey report in 2007, overall economic growth will continue to benefit India's poorer citizens and the deprived segment will shrink to 22% of the total population by 2025. The increase in disposable income and the shift from the "Deprived" income status to the middle class will boost demand and increase consumption. By 2025, India is expected to be among the world's top five consumer markets, surpassing Germany.

Knowledge and Business Processing Industry

The Indian technology and business services industry has experienced phenomenal growth in the past decade. It has been a conspicuous contributor to the Indian economy with $52 billion in revenues and employment for over 2 million people. It quadrupled its contribution to the GDP from 1 to 4% during the past decade. The industry has also contributed to the development of talent and education as well as spawning growth in ancillary and support services. Most of all, it has enhanced India's credibility as a business destination in quality round-the-clock service delivery. It has helped forge relationships with 75% of the Fortune 500 companies and generated immense savings for customers from global outsourcing.[39]

Services provided by BPO include call centers, telemarketing, finance, accounting, billing, database input and management, customer services, Human Resources (HR) management, logistics management, and even some front office management. Companies around the world are able to make huge savings in costs and focus on their core businesses by outsourcing some routine operations. Outsourcing evolved thereafter into the higher-end knowledge process outsourcing (KPO), which requires specialized expertise that India is able to provide due to its large pool of educated personnel. Services such as R&D, insurance, underwriting and risk assessment, financial analysis, data mining and analytics, business and market research, investment research, IP research, statistical analysis, tax preparation, engineering and design, animation and design, graphics simulation, writing and content development, network management, medical services, clinical trials, legal services, learning solutions, training, and consultancy are now being outsourced to India. Instead of only allowing cost savings solely through leveraging economies of scale and "rules based" process expertise, KPO accesses the global talent pool to carry out processes that demand specialized analytical and technical skills. The strategic driver for KPO is to add value by providing high quality business expertise and superior productivity through improved time to market in addition to realizing the traditional cost reductions through arbitrage of labor markets that made BPO so successful.

India has a tremendous pool of intellectual talent that has yet to be fully tapped. These highly-skilled workers and technically-educated professionals have developed specialized expertise and capacity to contribute to sectors such as finance, pharmaceuticals, healthcare, biotechnology, insurance, electronics, software, aerospace, automotive, textiles, industrial machinery, entertainment, media and publishing, education, law, and engineering. A number of U.S. businesses have already made successful forays into the KPO domain in India to leverage India's knowledge pool. These include GE, IBM, Microsoft, HP, Intel, Oracle, Cisco, Texas Instruments, Sun Microsystems, Philips, Motorola, JP Morgan, Citigroup, McKinsey, Goldman Sachs, Reuters, Morgan Stanley, United Airlines, Ford, General Motors, and Caterpillar. Pharmaceutical clinical research in particular has seen tremendous growth in investment. Global pharmaceutical companies such as AstraZeneca, GlaxoSmithKline, Pfizer, Novartis, and Eli Lilly have moved portions of their clinical drug testing to India. This has allowed them to accelerate the trial time and time to market new drugs, and offers potential cost savings of 40–60% compared with the United States. India has also amended and improved patent laws and process protection and is offering incentives ranging from tax holidays to duty exemptions. India has also accepted the International Conference on Harmonization Guidelines for Good Clinical Practices.[40]

The financial services sector is also benefiting from the talent pool. There has been tremendous growth in India as leading global financial institutions such as JP Morgan, Citigroup, Prudential, Goldman Sachs, and ABN AMRO continue offshoring high-end work either through delivery by affiliated legal entities in India or by unaffiliated pure-play third-party vendors. They are now offshoring high-end financial processes such as equity research, business intelligence, credit-risk analysis, and insurance claims processing. Three delivery models may be used. One is the "Captive KPO," which involves offshoring through affiliated legal entities in India. Another is the "Third Party KPO," which is contracting with unaffiliated third party vendors. And finally, there is the "Joint Venture KPO," which involves partnering with local entities to share control of local operations used for delivery of KPO services.[41]

The IT services sector has now stabilized and is entering the consolidation stage. Larger players are increasingly acquiring smaller companies to ramp up their revenue and client acquisition, to expand business segments and enhance geographical reach. The country's top IT firms are shuffling positions. They are Tata Consultancy Services (TCS), Infosys Technologies, Wipro Technologies, Cognizant Technologies, iGate, and Mahindra Satyam. The fast-growing domestic market is another feature of the industry. The domestic market is likely to grow rapidly, driven by major government initiatives such as increased spending on e-governance and increased thrust on technology adoption/upgrading across various government departments to bridge the digital divide. The government of India has enacted a National e-Governance Plan (NeGP), which creates a big opportunity for IT vendors to create an effective partnership. It has allocated $9 billion for investment in NeGP projects until 2014. Hundred percent foreign ownership is permitted in the ITeS industry in India. India's unique geographical position allows for leveraging time zone differences. The government has established a separate Ministry of Information Technology for this specific purpose. The country's basic cellular, paging, and Internet services have been privatized, which allows for competition and consequent reliability and efficiency.

Emerging Indian MNEs

In recent years, India has emerged as a major source of FDI amongst emerging economies such as China, Brazil, and Russia. Although Indian firms have been investing abroad for many years, it is only since the late 1990s that Outward Foreign Direct Investment (OFDI) flows have risen rapidly. This is due to dismantling of foreign exchange restrictions on capital transfers for acquisition of foreign ventures by Indian firms. As a result of the growth of outflows, the *stock* of OFDI rose from about $0.1 billion in 1990 to about $2 billion in 2000, and then to $13 billion in 2006 taking India to 5th place among outward investing emerging markets. Currently in 2012, it is estimated to be around $43 billion.[42] India ranks 4th in foreign acquisition by emerging economies after Singapore, the UAE, and Russia, and 21st in the world. Unlike the case of OFDI from China where more than two thirds of OFDI is state owned or state controlled, Indian OFDI is predominantly a private sector activity.

The drivers of Indian OFDI include the quest for new markets, acquisition of resources for production, access to labor and skills, improvement of their economies of scale through acquisitions and mergers, diversification, and augmentation of firm-specific or industry competitive advantages. Indian firms have tended to use cross-border Mergers and Acquisitions (M&As) as the main mode of entry into developed economies, and "greenfield" investments into developing ones.[43] Listed in Figure 2.9 are some of the largest outward investors from India.

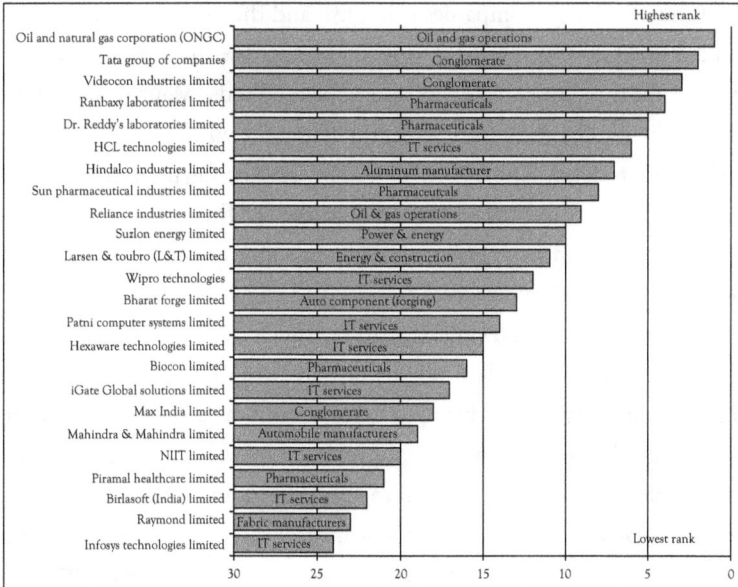

Figure 2.9. Largest outward investors from India by industries, 2006.

Source: Adapted from Economic Freedom of the States India 2011 [PDF version]. Retrieved February 25, 2012, from http://www.cato.org/economic-freedom-india/

Figure 2.9 allows for a broad understanding of Indian MNEs, their operations, and interests. The companies on the list were to be found in eight different industries. Judged by foreign assets, conglomerates dominate, with 37% of the aggregate assets. The oil and gas industry comes next with 33%, while pharmaceuticals are a somewhat distant third with 15%. Judged by the numbers of companies, IT is the leading industry on the list with eight companies, followed by pharmaceuticals with five, and then oil and gas and autos/auto parts with two each. Also represented are metals, power and energy, engineering and construction, and textiles.

Ten of the 24 selected MNEs were headquartered in Mumbai, four in Bangalore, and the rest in Aurangabad, Dehradun, Pune, Gurgaon, Noida, and New Delhi. Two of the 24 selected companies were listed on the London Stock Exchange, eight on the Luxembourg Stock Exchange, and four on the New York Stock Exchange and the Singapore Stock Exchange. Twenty-three out of 24 companies were also listed on an Indian Stock Exchange. One company, Birlasoft, was not listed anywhere. The official language of

23 of the 24 selected companies is English and the official language of Oil and Natural Gas Company (ONGC) is Hindi. The main destinations for Indian OFDI by 2009 were Singapore, Netherlands, Mauritius, Channel Islands, the United Kingdom, the United States, Cyprus, the UAE, Russia, Sudan, Switzerland, China, British Virgin Islands, Egypt, and Denmark. Indian OFDI is expected to continue growing. The sector and regional distribution of Indian OFDI is broadening due to the liberalization of such sectors as medical services, defense, and education.

Indian MNEs are now allowed to borrow abroad to finance overseas investments and to use domestic bank borrowing for the same purpose. This is prompting Indian firms to explore overseas acquisitions to build both domestic strength and global presence. In 2011, the Reserve Bank of India decided to further liberalize the overseas investment policy with a view to facilitate more operational flexibility in the corporate sector. Indian companies are now allowed to invest to the extent of 400% of the net worth of their bona fide businesses abroad, under an automatic route without further approval. They can further increase their exposure beyond 400% with prior approval from the Reserve Bank of India (RBI). Indian companies investing abroad will also be able to write off capital and other receivables like loans, royalty, technical know-how fees, and management fees of their joint ventures and wholly owned subsidiaries in which they have more than 51% stake.[44]

Many Indian firms use M&As to bring home new products and services and build competitive strength in India. They also seek international know-how and markets for their products. This is one method that international companies, especially Small and Medium Enterprises (SMEs), can use to enter the Indian market or represent or distribute Indian products and service in their home countries. The benefit would be availability of capital for investment in India, use of existing distribution channels of business partners, and faster access to the Indian market. This trend has been particularly evident for telecommunications (Tata Communications, Reliance Communications, Bharti Airtel, Essar Communications), energy (Oil and Natural Gas Corporation, Reliance Industries, Tata Power), infrastructure (GMR, DS Constructions), media, and entertainment (Reliance Entertainment), and agricultural firms (Karuthuri Global, Global Green, Renuka Sugars). Agricultural and resource investments are also being driven by mounting local resistance to large-scale projects involving community displacement and environmental disruption. India is expected to become the largest source of emerging market MNEs by 2024, with 20% more new MNEs than China, and over 2,200 Indian firms are likely to invest overseas in the next 15 years.[45]

Public Sector and State Owned Enterprises (SOEs)

India has had a large public sector controlled by the government. The number of SOEs in India increased 48-fold from 5 to 246 since India became independent in 1947. Total investments in 2009 reached approximately $106 billion as compared with only $6 million in 1951. The pre-independence SOEs were limited by the British to very few sectors including Railways, Posts and Telegraphs, Port Trusts, and Ordnance Factories. The agrarian economy was tarnished by vast income disparities, low level of savings, high unemployment, and regional disparity in economic development, poor infrastructure, a weak manufacturing base, inadequate capital, a poor entrepreneurship base, and a large unskilled labor base. In the absence of capital, the development of public sector enterprises was thus seen as a key driver to self-reliant economic growth.[46]

Trade liberalization started only in 1991 when both government and private enterprises consolidated their resources to compete on the global platform. The rise in the number of SOEs since the post-independence era was dominant in key industries such as agriculture, mining, manufacturing, electricity, and services. The role of SOEs varies according to the level of administration. India has a three-tier administration from the central government to state governments down to local level governments. There are different types of SOEs depending on the level of government. They consist of government companies, public corporations, departmental enterprises, public sector banks and institutions, cooperative societies, autonomous bodies, trusts, and deemed government companies.[47]

Privatization is in full swing. The key role of the government is to identify public sector enterprises and disinvest its interests to achieve overall managerial efficiency and increase productivity. It has relinquished up to 20% stake in the identified enterprises to strategic partners through a competitive bidding system (Figure 2.10). In March 1999, public sector enterprises were categorized as strategic (military, atomic energy, and railways) and non-strategic enterprises. The Indian government has also created the concept of *Maharatna, Navratna,* and *Miniratna* public sector enterprises to give them free rein in financial matters and managerial autonomy to incur capital expenditure and take part in joint ventures in domestic and foreign markets to increase their competitiveness against the private sector. In addition, the Indian government uses public sector enterprises as a medium to boost investments in areas where the private sector does not have the means to invest or it has little or no vested interests in the project. It develops economic policies through the public sector enterprises in order to shield the country from the impact of global economic crises.[48]

The disinvestments are evident in the amount of high proceeds realized between April 1992 and May 2008, which were approximately $10.7 billion. In 2009, market capitalization of 41 listed companies in the Bombay Stock Exchange (BSE) accounted for 26.4% of BSE market capitalization, compared with 21.8% in 2008. By 2009, market capitalization of listed companies had grown to 30%. According to a study conducted by Dun & Bradstreet India, SOEs' financial performance was better than that of private companies. In addition, SOEs contribute 40% of stock market profits predominantly in the sectors of energy and finance.[49]

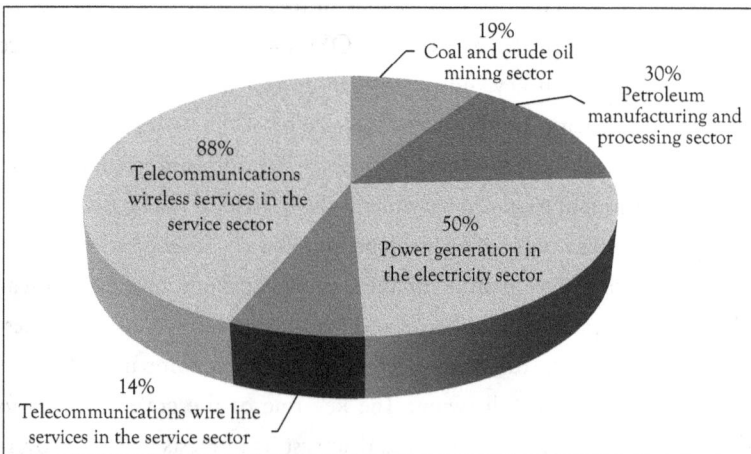

Figure 2.10. Share of private enterprises in public sector by percentage.

Source: Adapted from Indian Chamber of Commerce 2010. Retrieved January 4, 2012, from http://www.indianchamber.org/policy_forms/3.pdf

SOEs have become well-known companies in the international arena. For instance, Coal Company of India (CCI) is the largest coal producer in the world, ONGC ranks as the third largest oil and gas exploration and production (E&P) company in the world and 23rd among global energy companies. Although the government disinvested many of its interests to strategic partners, opportunities within the public sector continue to grow in the non-strategic enterprises. The wide range of activities include engineering, steel, heavy machinery, machine tools, fertilizers, drugs, textiles, pharmaceuticals, petrochemicals, extraction and refining of crude oil, and services such as telecommunication, trading, tourism, warehousing, and so forth and a range of consultancy services.[50]

Opportunities continue to grow within the private enterprises that participate in the public sector and they have gained a foothold in the four key industries dominated by the public sector enterprises. They are the coal and crude oil mining sector, petroleum in the manufacturing and processing sector, power generation in the electricity sector, and telecommunications in the services sector.

India's growing population and industrialization will lead to an increase in demand for coal-based electricity generation as the state-owned companies can only provide 90% of the electricity during peak-hour usage. This is a persistent problem facing businesses, particularly IT service providers, and forces them to look into acquiring their own power generators to tackle peak-hour power cuts.[51] Nevertheless, the power deficit, coupled with government decentralization in allowing private enterprises and foreign participation in this sector, provides numerous investment opportunities.

There are also tremendous opportunities to improve India's weak infrastructure such as airports, railways, and roads. Privatization has already begun with airports including those at Delhi, Mumbai, Hyderabad, Bangalore, and Cochin. This will boost tourism where India presently has a minute share in the global tourism market.[52] The defense (military) sector offers high growth potential in terms of defense equipment and IT systems, supply, and maintenance. In 2008 India was one of the biggest global military spenders, on par with Russia, Italy, Germany, and Japan. It imports approximately 70% of its defense equipment from overseas. The aim of the Indian government is to manufacture its military needs locally and thus create business opportunities for private enterprises and up to 26% FDI in this sector.

Family Owned Enterprises (FOEs)

FOEs have been present in India since ancient times but the modern Indian family business did not emerge until the mid-19th century, at the start of the Indian business era. Today, FOEs include small and medium enterprises and large public listed companies both locally and abroad. They normally survive two to four generations (Figure 2.11).[53] The nature of business they participate in is very wide and includes energy, chemicals, textiles, cement, metals, telecommunications, machinery, automobiles, finance, and hotel industries. Altogether, FOEs account for around 70% of the total sales and net profits of the biggest 250 private sector companies.

India was forced to open up its economy in the 1990s when it was hit by a serious economic crisis. Local businesses faced immense competition from foreign-owned firms that were technologically, managerially, and financially better equipped in every business sense. The resilient family owned firms, which survived a few generations, were able to adjust to the

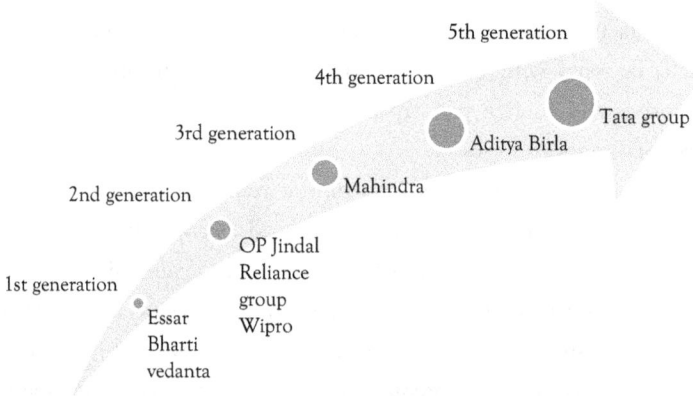

Figure 2.11. List of family owned enterprises by number of generations.

Source: Adapted from The Economist. (Data compiled from The Economist 2011). Retrieved October 30, 2011, from http://www.economist.com/node/21532449

changing market conditions. They made the necessary managerial changes and began to compete with and exist within the global scenario. They defied the general concept of confining their top executives' recruitment within their own family circle, a barrier that is very difficult to overcome due to the strong family values that are inherent in the Indian culture. Their willingness and openness to promote talent rather than blood relations and to go beyond their original industries are keys that helped them transform their family businesses into globally competitive firms.[54] One classic example of successful family-owned business is the internationally known Tata Group, which has a portfolio ranging from agriculture, IT, and consultancy services to manufacturing its own national car, the Tata Nano, known as the world's cheapest automobile.

FOEs have contributed significantly in providing employment to Indians. In addition, they produced the sixth richest man in the world, the CEO of the Adani Group.[55] FOEs began their own businesses as humble Indians but grew to achieve international presence by M&As with other big international conglomerates. Most top businesses in the world are FOEs but India's businesses have the highest percentage.[56]

They continue to work towards maintaining overall control by ensuring that the younger generations within the family are nurtured in their business acumen and develop influential leadership qualities. On the generation level, family constitutions have been set up to prevent sibling rivalry to avoid detrimental impact on the continuity of the global business. The trend in India is that family-owned businesses will continue to be passed on among the descendants of the family.[57] They are a great gateway to entry into the Indian market as most are well established with strong reputations and brand loyalty, diversified in numerous industries, are long-term oriented, and make excellent business partners.

CHAPTER 3

Mitigating Risks and Navigating Pitfalls

There are as many risks of doing business in India as there are opportunities. The economic potential is certainly unmatched but so is the complex business environment. The World Bank's *Doing Business 2012* profile ranks India at 134 in the world in "Ease of Doing Business" as compared with Japan 20, Mexico 53, China 91, Russia 120, Brazil 126, and Indonesia 129 (Figure 3.1). "While this ranking tells much about the business environment in an economy, it does not tell the whole story."[1]

India's advantages include a bustling democracy, a functioning and well-established civil service that is free of political influence, a strong rule-of-law tradition, more vigorous patent protection, better English

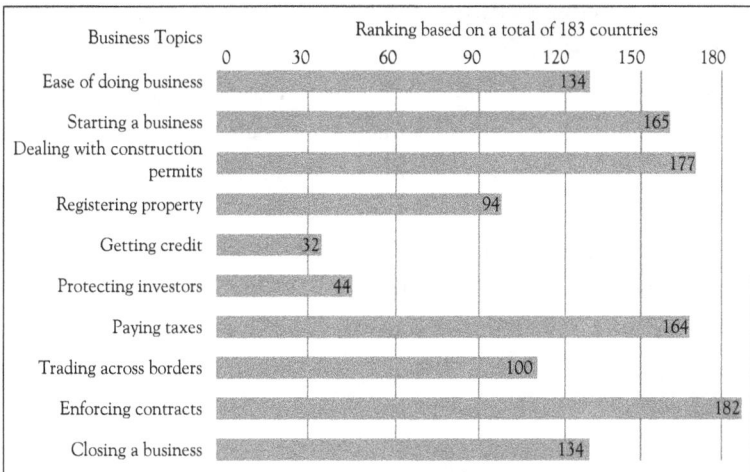

Figure 3.1. How India ranks on doing business topics.

Source: Adapted from World Bank Report 2011 Doing Business in India 2011. Retrieved November 14, 2011, from https://www.iaccindia.com/userfiles/files/Doing%20Business%202011%20%20India%20%28World%20Bank%20Report%29.pdf

language proficiency, a younger (and eventually bigger) population, an economy led by domestic consumption rather than exports, an open exchange of ideas, and the largest pool of entrepreneurs outside the United States. Yet, these are only half-truths. The Indian political system is often paralyzed, India's bureaucracy is cumbersome and inefficient, corruption is endemic, legal processes are time consuming and often flawed, labor laws are antiquated and clearly impede hiring and firing, the labor movement is excessively demanding, and the taxation system is so intricate that a second economy flourishes. This chapter discusses some of the pitfalls that may be encountered while doing business in India. It also suggests ways of succeeding in India with a long-term approach.

Political Uncertainty and Intransigence

India's democracy remains a work in progress, despite it being around for 65 years, the country having gained independence in 1947. India's democratic experiment is far from complete and little progress has been made towards achieving political stability due to divisions, rivalries, infighting, and factionalism. India has too many fault lines within its parties and between and among its parties, and between national and regional institutions. There are dozens of special-interest political parties in virtually every state government, and dozens more in the national government, hardly an indication or reliable foundation of stable and competent governance. Coalition governments have had to constantly make concessions to demands of constituent parties and this inevitably leads to delays in decision making and even disruptions in planning and implementing of economic policies. India's polity is not dominated by a single left–right ideological axis but multiple crosscutting axes, left–right, secular–religious–communal, centralist–regional–autonomist, and a variety of caste bloc-based axes, varying regionally. An important part of the coalition game in India is not just the forging of alliances between existing parties but the breaking of parties into splinter groups to facilitate alliances. All major parties in India have undergone splits.[2]

Over the past two decades, India has had coalition governments at the center as well as in the states. Since 1967, at least 50 coalition governments have functioned in the Indian polity. On average these governments lasted for 26 months. The leadership of India has changed several times since 1996 and no single party has had absolutely majority at the federal level in this period. The current coalition-led central government came to power in May 2009. The incumbent prime minister of India Dr Manmohan Singh is heading a coalition government of 15 parties called the United Progressive Alliance (UPA). The present government has adopted policies and taken initiatives that support economic liberalization pursued by previous governments. Risks remain clear as factionalism continues to impede implantation of these policies. The clearest example of the negative effects of political intransigence was the furor in 2011 over opening the multi-brand retail sector to foreign investment. Following protests from the opposition and even coalition partners, the government had to backtrack on its decision to allow FDI in retail, and this led to a severe dip in retail stocks. The former prime minister of Malaysia even suggested that India needs less democracy and a stronger central government, "a remark that cut at the core of the current political stalemate over the decision to allow foreign direct investment in multi-brand retail."[3]

India is considered a part of the 20 *least peaceful countries* in the world along with Pakistan, Iraq, and Afghanistan. It is ranked as the 135th most peaceful country in the world, according to the 2011 Global Peace Index, an initiative of the Institute of Economics and Peace, which evaluates 153 countries based on the level of ongoing conflict, safety and security, and militarization. India is currently experiencing political instability in the form of a decades-old Maoist uprising in its countryside and its intermittent border battles in the Kashmir region with Pakistan. Terror activity is not concentrated in a particular region in India but has seeped into almost all areas of the country, starting from the north, with the perennial conflict of Jammu and Kashmir due to political and religious imbalances, to the northeast, where there are tensions between state governments, the central government, and the tribal people. Central India is infested with the Maoist insurgency, which has seen serious acts of violence.

India has enormous infrastructure limitations that anyone traveling from any airport in India to any city can attest to. India has underinvested in infrastructure for many years, leaving the country with pockmarked roads, creaky railroads, congested ports, and more than 40% of rural households without access to electricity. Poor infrastructure continues to be cited as a bottleneck to economic growth in India. The government plans to spend more than $1 trillion on infrastructure through 2017, thereby boosting manufacturing and opening up the interior to greater commerce. Again, progress is slow and it will be some time before the required quality infrastructure is available for efficient movement of people, goods, and services.

The political risk of doing business in India is rated at CRT4, which is "Acceptable" or "Moderate" and on par with Indonesia and Russia.[4] Elections are due only in 2014 and political instability has not changed India's economic course though it has delayed certain decisions relating to the economy. The political divide in India is not one of policy, but essentially of personalities. Economic liberalization (which is what foreign investors are interested in) has been accepted as a necessity by all parties including the Communist Party of India (Marxist), which is in line with global changes. Thus, political instability in India, in practical terms, poses no major risk to foreign investors. It must be noted that no policy framed by a past Indian government has been reversed by any successive government so far. Even if political instability may return in the future, chances of a reversal in economic policy are low indeed. As for terrorism, no terrorist outfit is strong enough to destabilize the state in a country as large and diverse as India where turmoil and activism of some sort is considered natural and a continuing state of affairs. It must be expected that things will move quite slowly in a complex business environment such as India's, and one needs to be patient and persevere for long-term gains.

Corruption and Bureaucratic Roadblocks

India's bureaucracy has been aptly labeled as Byzantine, medieval, complex, sluggish, and intricate. A report by the Hong Kong based Political and Economic Risk Consultancy (PERC) found the Indian civil service to be the worst in Asia. It considered "Indian officialdom as the most stifling and most inefficient."[5] The survey was drawn from over 1,300 senior to middle level expatriate corporate executives from 12 Asian countries, who placed India's bureaucrats lower than Singapore, Hong Kong, Thailand, South Korea, Japan, Taiwan, Malaysia, China, Vietnam, the

Philippines, and Indonesia. The report confirmed that India's inefficient bureaucracy was largely responsible for most of the major complaints that business executives have about the country. A follow-up survey by *Babus of India* found that while one third of the respondents supported the PERC findings, another third voted that the Indian bureaucracy had in fact improved. However, if the view of another 26% respondents that it had in fact deteriorated is taken into account, 59% found that Indian bureaucracy has either deteriorated or is the worst in Asia.[6] Interestingly, the 2011–2012 Global Competitiveness Report of the World Economic Forum ranked India behind China but ahead of Russia and Brazil for the burden of government regulations as well as burden of customs procedures (Figure 3.2).[7]

India inherited an administration that was created by the British colonial rulers to serve the interests of the Queen and the British Parliament. The civil service put in place was designed to extract maximum revenues from the local Indians. Civil servants recruited and trained to perform this task were selected through a competitive examination held in London.

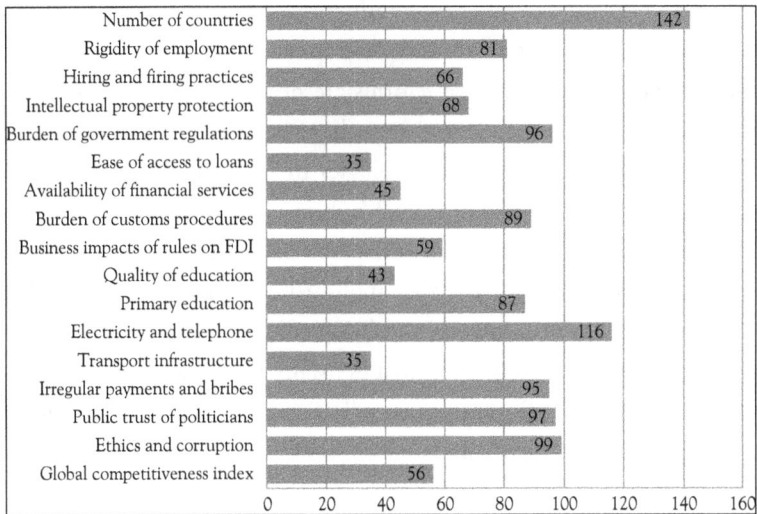

Figure 3.2. Global competitiveness index.

Source: Adapted from World Economic Forum, The Global Competitiveness Report, 2011–2012 (data compiled from The Global Competitiveness Report, 2011–2012). Retrieved February 18, 2012, from http://gcr.weforum.org/gcr2011/

Smart Indians who were hired to work as servants of the British government were made to feel superior to their brethren. Not much has changed with regards to the mindset, the structures of centralized administration, and cumbersome procedures designed to effect control in every form possible. India's bureaucracy today is bloated, slow moving, rigid and self-perpetuating. The red tape acts as an incentive for bribery. Indian bureaucracy is like a pyramid with a narrow top and a huge bottom with too many people doing too little work. The culture is one of a privileged class carrying an aura of apathy and rudeness. Not many are held accountable for their inefficiencies. Even in the investigation and prosecution of members of the service who have been charged with crimes, the system is notoriously slow. Indian bureaucracy has an impeccable record of protecting itself from change and responsibility such that disciplinary action is diluted to the point of meaninglessness. Worst of all, Indian civil servants work hand-hand with corrupt politicians.

However, things are changing rapidly. Public outcry against the poor quality of public service has grown in recent years and people are demanding more transparency and accountability. The success of the private sector in the provision of services has also been a factor in the demand for reform and the need to find new solutions to an age-old problem. If India is to sustain its high growth and development over the coming years, comprehensive administrative reforms are needed, and fast. A series of Administrative Reforms Commissions have been working to streamline the Indian bureaucracy. New technologies are being used to increase efficiency, reduce red tape, and prevent bribery. There has been restructuring and reshuffling of government departments and agencies too. Many administrative positions have been abolished, redesigned, or renamed to cut down the size of ministries and bring efficiency and effectiveness in administrative operations and activities. Many sectors have been deregulated and concerted efforts at decentralization are being made. Licensing is being reduced drastically. Indian civil servants are being better paid and held more accountable.

Despite all this, red tape continues to be cited as a major deterrent to investing and doing business in India. Even returning Indians continue to complain about the obstacles and day-to-day hassles of getting things done. One must be prepared to deal with these "minor" inconveniences for long-term gains. Things are improving, not as fast as many would like, but the reality of slow progress has to be contended with. Many companies are finding it worth their while.

Corruption is present in every aspect of public life in India and exists at all levels. At the higher level there are scams like the recent telecom case, dubbed the 2G Spectrum Scam, that cost the government an estimated $39 billion in revenue when mobile licenses were awarded to companies too cheaply in return for a large payoff. There is a long history of such high-level scams and even a top 10 spam list including the Bofors scam (military kickbacks), Commonwealth Games scam (discrepancies in project tenders and payment to non-existent parties), fodder scam (subsidy of fictitious livestock), Satyam scam (fudging of corporate books), IPL scam (sports franchise), and *hawala* scam (money paid to politicians through *hawala* traders). Then there is petty corruption, such as middlemen taking a cut as they distribute subsidized food to the poor. Most shockingly, there is corruption at the heart of the electoral system: candidates pay cash to voters to attend their rallies and even to vote for them.[8]

A 2005 study done by Transparency International (TI) in India found that more than 50% of people had firsthand experience of paying bribes or peddling influence to get a job done in a public office. On TI's 2011 corruption perception index, India scored 3.1 on a scale from zero to 10, where anything below five is bad news. The TI study brings together recent data from a variety of sources, including business surveys and country experts, to assess the overall extent of graft in 183 nations. India was ranked 95th, way lower than China, Asia's other major fast-growing economy, which scored 3.6 points and ranked 75th. Of the Brazil, Russia, India, China (BRIC) economies, India did better than only Russia, which ranked way down at 143 with a score of 2.4. In the South Asian region, India did worse than both Sri Lanka (86) and the tiny Himalayan kingdom of Bhutan (38). Still, India did better than Pakistan (134) and Nepal - the South Asian country where corruption is perceived as most widespread - at 154. At the very bottom of the list were Afghanistan, Myanmar, North Korea, and Somalia, which fared worst of all. India's score has been slowly eroding since 2007, with the latest downgrade the most dramatic.[9]

India's fight against corruption has been led on numerous fronts and surprisingly, much progress has been made in the last few years. At the highest level has been the Supreme Court addressing the issue of corruption in rulings and lambasting the government for failing to take action. On its part the government is under extreme pressure to act and has done so in announcing sweeping reforms to come. The biggest move is toward passing the *Jan Lokpal Bill*, (Citizens' Ombudsman Bill) which is a draft anti-corruption bill drawn by prominent civil-society activists seeking the appointment of a Jan Lokpal, an independent body that would investigate corruption cases and complete the investigation within a year. It envisages completion of the trial in the case within the next year. It was finally passed by the Lower House (Lok Sabha) on December 28, 2011 due to public pressure and fasts by the leader of the anti-corruption movement, Anna Hazare. For it to be implemented, a constitutional amendment is necessary. Other measures the government is planning include state funding for political parties, the removal of discretionary powers abused by politicians and civil servants, and the ratification of a UN corruption convention.[10]

Interestingly, many initiatives at the grassroots level are having immediate effects. Technology has been the tool providing innovative solutions. A website (www.ipaidabribe.com) was created in 2010 to allow people to post details of how they were forced to bribe. Within seven months over 5,000 reports were lodged. The expectation is that when Indians are better informed they will feel more empowered and refuse to pay. The results have been impressive. Someone in Karnataka admitted shame for paying $4 to pass a driving test; in Mumbai it costs $20 to register a baby; and Bangalore's transport commissioner likes the site as it allows him to see how corrupt his junior officials have become. In Gujarat, a tendering system has been put in place where companies bid on public contracts online, ensuring transparency. A system was created five years ago where homeowners can assess their property tax online instead of having corrupt inspectors visit their homes. Villages are being hooked up to broadband and to state databases. Farmers can now print their land title deeds in two minutes and at minimal cost of about 20 cents and apply for financing from nearby banks quickly. In the past it would have taken days and also depended on the whim of a civil servant. Buying train tickets is a cinch, now that it is all computerized.

The Right to Information (RTI) Act passed in 2006 has been a game changer. Until 2005, an ordinary citizen had no access to information held by a public authority, even in matters affecting legal entitlements. A citizen now has the legal right to information about the details of public policies and expenditures, what process has been followed in designing the policies affecting them, how the programs have been implemented, who are the concerned officials associated with the decision making process and execution of the schemes, and why the promises made for delivery of essential services to the poor have not been fulfilled. Lack of openness in the functioning of the government provided a fertile ground for breeding inefficiency and lack of accountability in the working of the public authorities, which in turn, perpetuated all forms of corruption. Now, all public authorities have to place information in the public domain and the citizen has the right to observe what is going on inside an organization. There is greater transparency than before in the working of public bodies. Applications for information have grown ten-fold. Government at all levels is being made more accountable as a response in 30 days or less is mandatory.

Locals, returning Indian businesspeople, and professionals, as well as foreigners have highlighted India's shortcomings in terms of lack of transparency and governance that have been breeding corrupt practices. Investors have cited these inefficiencies as having caused their withdrawal from India. Home legislation against bribery for U.S. and European corporations as well as the general attitude of international companies not to engage in or encourage corrupt practices has had a meaningful impact on developing countries such as India. In response to this, the Indian Cabinet has approved The Prevention of Bribery of Foreign Public Officials and Officials of Public International Organizations Bill, 2011 (also called the *Foreign Bribery Bill*) making it an offence for foreigners to bribe local officials. It has also decided to amend the Indian Penal Code (IPC) to make private sector bribery a criminal offence. Both these laws, when enacted, will go a long way in dealing with the endemic problem and in making it more palatable for foreign business people. For the many foreign companies that are continuing to enter India, this is already the case. It is best not to offer a bribe to get any job done, not only because it is wrong, but it is illegal as well.

It is possible to do business in India without engaging in corruption and most companies are already doing it.

Winding Web of Litigation: Enforcing Contracts, Paying Taxes, and Protecting Intellectual Property

The Indian legal system, a British legacy, is sound and well structured. Based on English law, India has a common law-based legal system, under which India's basic commercial laws are similar to those of other Commonwealth jurisdictions including the United Kingdom, Canada, Australia, New Zealand, Singapore, and Hong Kong. The Indian legal system is therefore based on a combination of legislation and judicial precedent, also known as case law. India is a constitutional republic with a partly federal system of governance. As in the United States, legislation is passed both at the federal and state levels. For this reason, there are plenty of legislations and authorities, which make the practice of Indian law both complex and well laid out.

But the system is badly broken. Corruption is a major cause of breakdown of the Indian legislative process. The *2011 Business Anti-Corruption* portal reports, "the judiciary, particularly at the lower levels, is reportedly rife with corruption. Most citizens have great difficulty securing effective and fair case resolution through the courts. Citizens report that court procedures are very slow and complicated and that the court system fuels the use of bribes and other kinds of influence-peddling. People give bribes to obtain a favorable judgment, but bribes are also used to influence public prosecutors." This is further illustrated by the Transparency International's *Global Corruption Barometer 2010*, in which a substantial number of household respondents reported having paid a bribe to the judiciary. According to the US Department of State 2010, bribes are reportedly paid to move a case more rapidly through the system.[11]

India's legal system is seriously overburdened. The backlog of cases is astounding. According to the Chief Justice of India, it would take the Delhi High Court 466 years just to clear its backlog of criminal cases. India has only 11 judges for every million people compared with roughly 110 per million in the United States. There are easily 600 cases that are more than 20 years old. The United Nations Development Program estimates that some 20 million legal cases are pending in India. As a result, it is not uncommon to hear stories of court cases lasting longer than the average human lifespan. In 2011, the Indian government approved an ambitious program aimed at the disposal of pending cases in three years, from the current average of 15 years. Known as the "National Mission for Justice Delivery and Legal Reforms," it seeks to operationalize a number of plans to ensure expeditious and quality justice.[12] Though India's courts are notoriously inefficient, they at least comprise a functioning independent judiciary and the rule of law generally prevails. The Indian Supreme Court remains fiercely independent.

Enforcing Contracts

According to data collected by the World Bank, enforcing a contract in India requires 46 procedures, takes 1,420 days, and costs around 40% of the value of the claim. Globally India stands at 182 in the ranking of 183 countries on the ease of enforcing contracts.[13] The most common advice given by Indian lawyers to international businessmen is not to litigate but to seek an alternative dispute resolution (ADR) or even settle. The Indian Arbitration and Conciliation Act, 1996 is the governing arbitration statute in India. It is based on the Model Law on International Commercial Arbitration adopted by the United Nations Commission on International Trade Law (UNCITRAL) in 1985. However, arbitration is also considered to be cumbersome and time consuming, so other ADR methods such as mediation, negotiation, and out-of-court settlements are the more palatable solutions.

Taxation

Bloomberg reports that tax evasion is a national sport in India. Uncollected taxes amount to $314 billion annually.[14] The Indian tax system remains overtly complex both at the central and state levels. The most significant cause of complexity is policy-related and is due to the existence of exemptions and multiple rates, and the extant structure of the levies. There is excessive emphasis on indirect taxation. There is excise duty (for manufactured goods), central sales tax collected by the federal government, state sales tax on local sales, a value-added tax for multi-point sales and service tax that is payable by service providers. India is planning to implement a dual goods and services tax (GST) system, which would be levied at a single point. In this GST system, both central and state taxes will be collected at the point of sale. All goods and services, barring a few exceptions, will be brought into the GST base. There will be no distinction between goods and services. This system is expected to be implemented in June 2012.[15]

India stands 147th in a ranking of 183 countries on the ease of paying taxes. On average, firms make 33 tax payments a year, spend 254 hours a year filing, preparing, and paying taxes, and pay total taxes amounting to 24.7% of profit. However, reforms have been set in place by the government to ease the paying of taxes. In 2011, it reduced the administrative burden of paying taxes by abolishing the fringe benefit tax and improving electronic payment. In 2012, it eased the burden of paying taxes for firms by introducing mandatory electronic filing and payment for value added tax.[16] A new Direct Tax Code is due to come into effect in 2013 and aims at reducing tax rates by expanding the tax base and minimizing exemptions. Professional help will be needed to deal with tax issues in India.

Intellectual Property Rights (IPR)

India has been a member of the WTO since 1995. This requires member nations to establish intellectual property (IP) laws whose effect is in line with minimum standards. They cover patents, trademarks, copyrights, industrial designs, and geographical indications. India's Patents Act of 1970 and 2003 Patent Rules set out the law concerning patents and there is no provision for utility model patents and operates under the "first to file" principle. India's trademark laws consist of the 1999 Trade Marks Act and the Trade Marks Rules of 2002, which became effective in 2003. Trade names also constitute a form of trademark in India, with protection, irrespective of existing trade names, for those wishing to trade under their own surname. India is a signatory to the Berne Convention on copyright and this protects written or published works such as books, songs, films, Web content and artistic works. The laws governing designs are the Designs Act 2000 and the Designs Rules 2001, and designs are valid for a maximum of 10 years, renewable for a further five years. However, India is not a party to either the 1996 World Intellectual Property Organization (WIPO) Copyright Treaty (WCT) or the WIPO Performances and Phonograms Treaty (WPPT).

A major concern is the lack of protection against unfair commercial use of "test or other data that companies submit to the government in order to obtain marketing approval for their pharmaceutical and agricultural chemical products."[17] Companies in India are able to copy certain pharmaceutical products and seek immediate government approval for marketing based on the original developer's data. Piracy of copyrighted materials remains a problem in India. The system of filing trademarks under the Madrid Protocol is expected to be implemented by the Indian Intellectual Property Office by 2012 and an electronic filing system for trademarks has been introduced. It is important to note that India restricts the use of trademarks by foreign firms unless they invest in India or supply technology. The Indian Constitution delegates enforcement to state governments and often this is not done. India's criminal justice system also does not effectively support the protection of IP. A bill is pending in the Upper House of the Indian Parliament, which specifically deals with all commercial disputes including IP cases.

It is best to seek legal advice before embarking on any business venture and to retain professional help in dealing with compliance, contractual, and tax issues in advance. Such services are readily available and not prohibitive in terms of costs when compared with western countries.

Employment and Human Resources Limitations

Although India's 520-million-strong labor force is the second largest in the world (2010), there exists a dire labor shortage. The unemployment rate is 9–10%. The total labor force amounts to just 35.9% of its population of 1,182 million in 2009–2010 and 74% remain in the rural areas. According to a series of surveys (2009–2010) by the Labor Bureau, India's labor market "not only displays many features of a pre-modern economy, but reflects a growing inability to absorb its large, young and still growing labor force."[18] India is clearly far from exploiting the "demographic dividend" offered by a younger population. It is estimated that only about 8% of India's population is employed in the formal/organized sector (government and corporates), which contributes a whopping 60% to the national GDP. Shockingly, 94% of the total labor force is in the unorganized sector. This amounts to 433 million workers, accordingly to the National Sample Survey Organization (NSSO) and was announced by the Labor and Employment Minister in the Upper House in 2011.[19] Unorganized labor is informal labor whose use is not governed either by state regulations or by collective agreements between workers and employers. These include agriculture workers, migrant workers, causal laborers, self-employed, building and construction workers, taxi drivers, domestic workers, fishermen, vendors and more. Whatever skills they have are acquired outside the formal education system.

Only about 10% of the workforce in the country has some form of skill training (2% with formal training and 8% with informal training). This is extremely low when compared with countries like Korea (96%), Germany (75%), Japan (80%), and the United Kingdom (68%). Women's participation in the labor market is also low in India. There is also a continuing migration of skilled people in search of better opportunities overseas. In 2012, a shortfall of 3 million skilled workers is estimated. India's construction industry had about 31.5 million workers, 83% of them unskilled, in 2005.[20] To help tackle the shortage, construction companies have set up their own training schools to train carpenters, electricians, and construction equipment operators. The FICCI Survey on Labor also confirmed that "labor and skill shortage continues to be one of the key concerns for the Indian industry."[21] Ninety percent of the participating companies indicated that they are unable to find adequate numbers of workers for running their operations.

India's labor laws are overlapping, inconsistent, and cumbersome. They have their roots in colonial rule and were last fully updated in the Industrial Disputes Act of 1947 (that mandates government permission for closure of enterprises employing more than 100 workers), the Industrial Employment (Standing Orders) Act, 1946 (that, inter alia, mandates workers' consent prior to re-designating or relocating their jobs again in enterprises with 100 or more workers), and the Contract Labor (Regulation and Abolition) Act, 1970 (that prohibits employment of contract labor in core and perennial activity of the enterprises).[22] An additional

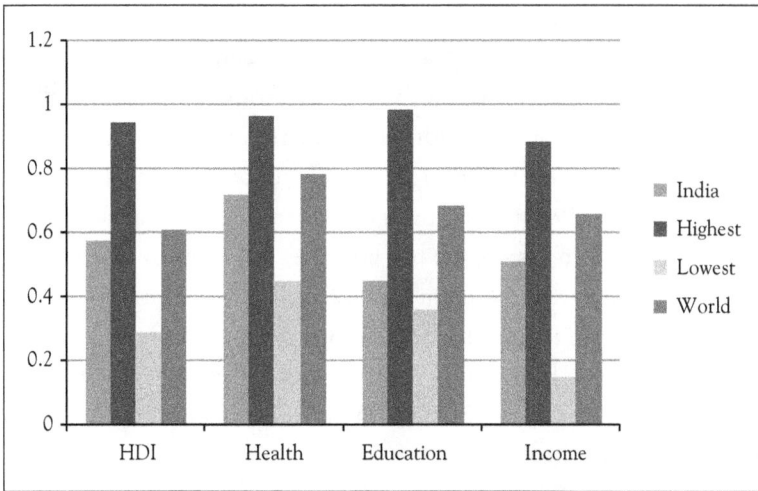

Figure 3.3. Human development index.

Source: Adapted from World Economic Forum, The Global Competitiveness Report, 2011–2012 (data compiled from The Global Competitiveness Report, 2011–2012). Retrieved February 18, 2012, from http://gcr.weforum.org/gcr2011/

45 national laws intersect or derive from the 1948 Act, and about 200 state laws control the relationships between employees and employers. Companies must keep six attendance logs and 10 separate accounts for overtime wages, and file five types of annual returns. Some labor laws were waived starting in 2001 to encourage growth in the IT sector, India's second-largest earner of foreign exchange, by placing most of the workforce inside fenced-off zones. The waivers allowed IT companies and call centers to operate 24 hours a day, recruit women to work late at night without building single-gender facilities, and add staff freely without submitting layoff decisions to the authorities. Flexibility in hiring and firing is not the only problem; India's complex web of legislation leads to a system of dispute resolution that is incredibly slow. There are thousands of disputes pending in India's labor courts, and of these 28,864 had been pending for over 10 years. India could have added 2.8 million jobs to the formal economy in the decade through 2007 had labor laws been less restrictive, the World Bank said in 2007.

The Indian workforce is the most "mentally mobile" in the world - a measure of the willingness of the country's employees to change jobs. India's mobility index was highest, followed by Mexico, China, and

Turkey. The lowest mobility is in Luxembourg, Italy, and Hungary. Employees in Bangalore are the most mobile, and more than 80% of the Indians surveyed are certain about the prospects of finding a different job in the short term. Although India's Constitution guarantees workers right to form unions, India's trade union movement has been in decline since 1992.[23] India's trade union movement has a long history of activism and work stoppage but now the tide seems to have turned. Permanent employees are often laid off in favor of contract workers. This is in response to laws that are so protective of workers that they are an impediment to hiring and growth. Managers say that the country's complex web of federal and state laws that are intended to protect permanent workers "are so onerous that few employers want to hire them. They cover virtually every aspect of employment—how workers are hired, what they are paid, how many hours they can work and whether they can be fired."[24] The productivity of Indian workers is among the lowest of major Asian countries and companies are using automation to reduce their dependence on large labor forces and to improve efficiency. The Indian labor force is, however, easy to train, labor is abundant, and unskilled workers easy to find and rather inexpensive. Payroll costs run in the range of 20–40% of total production. Indian companies are outsourcing their own jobs within their own country. These part-time workers may be paid half of what permanent employees earn and receive fewer benefits. Foreign companies complain about the tedium of processing payroll and benefits paperwork and are beginning to rely on contract hiring agencies, though they may be reluctant to say so publicly. Easily 25% of industrial laborers work on contract and even government agencies rely on temporary employees. Foreign companies that come to India often hire law firms and staffing agencies before hiring anyone else.

India's Ubiquitous Second Economy

Often termed as "black" and "number two", India has had a second economy running parallel to the main "white" and "number one" for a long time now. It is huge and its worth is estimated at 40–60% of the country's GDP - valued in excess of $500 billion. The money transaction is called "black" money as it as the result of corruption, crime, and other "sins" and remains underground so as to evade taxes as well. This was acknowledged even by the government's Central Statistical Organization (CSO), which estimated tax lost on account of black money at around $225 billion a year.[25] The estimated costs of this to the economy are said to total $9 trillion, based on an estimated 5% of GDP growth sacrificed every year since the mid-1970s when *Emergency Rule* prevailed and government price and production controls ruled. Accordingly to researcher Professor Arun Kumar of the Center for Economic Studies, Jawaharlal Nehru University, New Delhi, per-capita income could have been seven times larger, the economy could have become the second largest in the world, and India would have become a middle income country and not remained one of the poorest.[26]

The *formal* economy consists of businesses that pay taxes, adhere to labor regulations, and burnish the country's global image. India's *informal* economy is everything else. It exists largely outside government oversight, is cash-based, involves unreported transactions off the books and with no records, is generated by both legal and illegal activities, involves cross-border movement of funds, and is responsible for as much as 90% of all employment.[27] Real estate deals are struck in Indian currency abroad and in India, at least 40% of the money transacted in real estate is black as the money is unaccounted for, and most taxation is avoided. Even transfer of title deeds is replaced by power of attorney documentation to avoid paying sales tax and transfer fee and this goes on for generations. It is said that "an Indian is affected at every step of the black economy. The education of a child, a visit to a doctor, policemen who extort money, daily purchases, electricity or water departments all demand black payments."[28]

Just the pilfering of electricity is costly and hurting growth. The Indian Secretary of Power reports that at least one third of the 174 GW of electricity generated annually is either stolen or gets dissipated by the conductors and transmission equipment that form the distribution grid. That is more than any other nation in the world - in China the rate was only 8% in 2010. The pilfering of almost enough power to charge California for a year lowers India's yearly economic output of $1.3 trillion by 1.2%, says India's Planning Commission.[29]

A huge chunk of illicit funds are kept in banks abroad. In 2011, spurred by public criticism of its poor handling of black money and the Supreme Court's intervention, the Indian government revealed that tax authorities had secured leads from foreign banks involving 9,900 suspicious overseas transactions involving Indian citizens. In two years, the Directorate of International Taxation collected over $700 billion in taxes from cross-border transactions.[30] As recently as February 2012, the Central Bureau of Investigation (CBI), India's premier law enforcement agency for the investigation of corruption, admitted, "Indians are the largest depositors in banks abroad with an estimated $500 billion of illegal money stashed by them in tax havens. Largest depositors in Swiss banks are also reported to be Indians."[31]

The government is amending double tax agreements with 81 countries to counter this. The quantum of illegal funds abroad is estimated between $500 million and $1.5 trillion but no confirmation is possible. In 2009, the German government passed on to their Indian counterparts names and bank account details of 18 Indians who had stashed their "ill-gotten wealth" in the LGT Bank of Liechtenstein. The Indian government could not disclose the names of the individuals as the information was obtained under a "secrecy clause." A large part of the black money is also generated through transfer pricing mechanism. A special committee has been set up under the Central Board of Direct Taxes (CBDT) to deal with this problem.[32]

The costs of the black economy are huge. Bribes are induced by the bureaucrats to "speed up" services as roadblocks were first created to demand payments. The administration focuses on devising ways to work inefficiently. This has spawned a culture of "middlemen" and "personal approaches" to resolve issues that should have been solved as part of the services provided. The bribe giver also needs the middlemen to get this done as he does not know how much to give and to whom. Foreigners are approached by middlemen to speed up the processes of permits and approvals. Court cases are unnecessarily delayed, causing unnecessary backlog, and payment is required to move forward. All this affects macro and micro-level planning at the federal and state levels. Monetary and fiscal policies do not achieve desired results. Targets for public services are not met as "expenditures do not meet outcomes." Direly needed capital is sent abroad or tied down in gold or real estate. This makes the country capital-shy and affects development, growth, and employment creation as well as creating a shortfall in education and public services.[33]

The implementation of the GST system and the digitization of records and transaction is a big blow to the black economy. Strict government action and the drive towards transparency are also making life difficult for those operating in the black economy. An even stronger political will is needed to curb black activity completely. Foreign businessmen are duly urged to avoid making any black transactions, as the costs are most likely to be not worth the risk.

CHAPTER 4

Relationship Building and Partnering in India

India's complexity exists not only in its structures and processes but most of all in its people. When asked about what stood out most in his visit to India, an Englishman once responded that it was "the Indians." The key to success in India lies not only in anticipating business roadblocks, but also in understanding the way Indians think and view the world. India is a country where relationships are placed before business and thus the relationship phase of the business process should be considered the most important. In numerous ways, cultural differences influence every area of business relationships, interactions, processes, and systems. It is imperative to understand these differences as they enable risk mitigation and development of strategies that avoid pitfalls. This chapter highlights this and outlines possible approaches in dealing with Indians in building workable relationships with partners and associates.

Understanding the Indian Psyche

The Indian psyche remains an enigma to the Western mind. Indian culture is certainly complex with traditions and value systems that have been in place for thousands of years. A comprehensive understanding of Indian culture and worldview requires a holistic and integrated approach. Indian society is multifaceted to an extent unknown elsewhere. Mark Twain in his exposé *Following the Equator* noted, "So far as I am able to judge, nothing has been left undone, either by man or nature, to make India the most extraordinary country that the sun visits on his rounds. Nothing seems to have been forgotten, nothing overlooked." Virtually no generalizations can be made for all the groups and subgroups that make up Indian society. The cultural complexity has been colored by the multitude of immigrations, invasions, colonial rule, and modernization that have brought with them streams of alien influences, only parts of which were assimilated into the primordial Indian worldviews; while the remaining ones coexist within the overreaching Indian worldviews.[1]

Religion pervades all life in India and the social and religious structures have defined the nation's identity for more than 5,000 years. Indian society has been structured mainly by the Hindu religion, which is rooted in ritual, castes, a pantheon of gods, and reincarnation. Hinduism has endured numerous foreign influences and the evolution of new religions. It is not unexpected that religion directly influences the essential Indian personality and value system. As a comparison, it has been posited that while the Chinese are situation-centered, and Americans individual-centered, Indians are supernaturally centered. The Indian mind is characterized by three major themes. First, *cosmic collectivism* reflects a worldview that the universe consists of diverse forms of animate and inanimate elements that are compatible as well as conflicting, but are all interconnected and held together as part of the ultimate reality, the *Brahman*. Next, the whole cosmos and everything within it is arranged in a *hierarchical order* of being. As such animates are superior to inanimates, and humans are superior to both. Among human beings, hierarchical order is based on castes and within castes on age and gender. Within a human being, the head is superior to the middle parts of the body, which are superior to the feet. The body itself has five layers from the gross body being the lowest to the subtle body (the soul or *atman*) being the highest. Even food, weather, states of mind, and all conceivable phenomena have layers of hierarchy. Finally, *spirituality* is built into the Indian psyche even though animal impulses and worldly material strivings are very much a part of life. Human endeavor requires living with these and working towards transcending them toward perfection through detachment between body and mind as well as between states of mind.[2]

These conflicting demands from contrasting dispositions and orientations are held together in Hindu thoughts as laid out in the ancient texts, the *Upanishads*. The world can be partitioned into opposites and then put together into one whole, and then partitioned again. People who have a worldview that can deal with such a system of logic are likely to define problems differently and even use different methods to analyze and solve the problems selected. Thus, according to the ancient Indian worldview, people tend to work toward attaining the unattainable. This inevitably results in a strong moral orientation and often a lack of pragmatism. Achievement goals would as such include considering the well-being of others, seeking the respect of and respecting others, especially elders, and observing to the letter social codes of conduct.[3]

This, to an extent, explains the ability of Indians to live with abounding paradoxes. Inconsistency and contradictions constitute a core of the Indian mindset. For example, Indians are primarily collectivist, but each has a well-protected secret individualist self, complete with thoughts, feelings, and aspirations. As individualists, Indians are very goal-oriented and aggressive, much like Westerners but simultaneously, they are strongly family oriented and will confine their loyalties to the very few that are close to them. They are Easterners on the one hand and as a result of many years of external influence, have adopted Western values. These paradoxes are reflected in many ways.[4] Indians pride themselves as being pure and clean yet there is rubbish strewn everywhere, except in places of worship. Well-groomed individuals will dump their trash right outside their homes. The cleanliness of the entire country falls way short of Western standards. The wealthy and the poor live side-side all over the country and feel nothing for the other. The well-fed shopkeeper orders around his scrawny help. The way things are is quite readily accepted and accommodated. What others think of you and how you act matters more than your own personal viewpoints. Very often what is said and what is done are not congruent as the public face is given high priority. As a Western manager explains, "I feel that the most difficult thing is that the Indians will tell you one thing, think another, and do another thing, which is not what we would do."[5]

The social interdependence of Indians is a theme that pervades life. The notion is that everything one does involves interaction with other people: families, clans, sub-castes, castes, and religious affiliations, which include divine beings in the supernatural realm. This involves constant attention and participation in the social nexus, requiring attention to hierarchy, respect, honor, the feelings of others, rights and obligations, hospitality, and gifts of food and clothing, jewelry, and cash. Also required is commitment of time to maintain these relationships, which is usually at the expense of work and productivity. The assumption is that social relationships can further one's position in life and not doing so will result in failure. These ties have been carried from past lives and will continue to the next. Loyalty to family, clan, and community takes precedence and continues to be a deeply held ideal for almost everyone. Friends, family members, and relatives are trusted and favored. Strangers and out of group individuals are distanced, mistrusted, and discriminated against.[6]

Indians have a very unique persona. They tend to exaggerate their claims and present themselves to know it all. Often uttered statements such as "No problem" and "*achcha, ho jayega*" (yes, it will be done) may result in loss of trust and damage relationships with foreigners, who may hold them to higher performance standards. Indians can also be poor listeners as being vocal has been their national trait. They tend to show superior knowledge and express personal opinions readily. Indians "speak eloquently about topics they know nothing about," observed an early visitor Al Beruni in 1017 AD. Indians are also wont to wash their dirty linen in public when matters once considered private come out in the open, to the detriment of the parties involved. In principle, though, Indians do tend to be secretive especially with regard to family and business matters as is the general tradition in Asia.[7]

Selecting Partners and Appointing Agents

Joint ventures remain the most preferred form for investing and operating in India. Other options include setting up a *liaison office* where the foreign party can get a feel of the Indian market but the actual business is done from the home country; a *branch office* can be set up in India but this would have adverse tax consequences (high income tax rate of 40%); setting up a *project office* if only one project is being performed in India; establishing a *limited liability partnership;* appointing a *distributor;* and establishing a *wholly owned subsidiary* (WOS) in India. India is virtually a tax haven for those wishing to set up a manufacturing and export base. Therefore, 100% export-oriented units either in the form of a WOS or a joint venture should be given due consideration. The selection of mode of entry would naturally be based on considerations covering industry, short- and long-term goals, control desired, local partner's contribution and equity, tax exposure, protection of IP and corporate information and structure of company, and partnership or joint working arrangements.

Selection of the right partner remains the key to success in India. It will be a serious mistake to jump into business without really getting to know the Indian partner. You must be comfortable with the other party and find it easy to communicate, express your opinions, ideas and expectations and the corporate culture must be well understood and recognized. Databases are readily available as a means of selecting business partners matching one's requirements. These lists cover distributors, sales specialists, technical specialists, manufacturers, resellers, and integrators depending on the type of industry one is looking at. Business in India is done at a very personal level. While in the West *networking* is considered an additional advantage in business collaboration, in India it is the essential method of establishing a business venture. Indian culture requires establishing a *personal relationship* before any form of cooperative venture can be initiated. Indians rely on personal "connections" to help them move forward in life. This is learned very early in life and forms the basis of all social and professional activity. Family is the crux of this network and is expanded to include relatives, friends, colleagues, and members of the community. Making use of this network to get what you want in life is embedded in the DNA of most Indians. The network is passed on through parents and is furthered through marriage. This network helps them to get into schools, social groups, jobs, ownership of property, and finding partners for siblings and children. Trust has to be earned and a track record set. Upon being introduced, the Indian begins slowly to check you out within the network to establish your standing, reliability, reputation, and status. All this means that it will take some time before a comfort zone is found for two parties to work together for mutual benefit.

On your part, due diligence and risk assessment becomes a major undertaking. Net worth, credit, and reputation checks are becoming easier now with many professional organizations providing these services. Even established players are known to have exaggerated their capabilities. At first glance, many potential agents or partners may appear to have excellent credentials and industry contacts. As has been explained earlier, the Indian propensity to exaggerate needs to be taken into account when deciding whom to do business with. They would typically claim to be more than they usually are. It is important to resist the temptation to establish a relationship merely because the Indian party is persistent or the keenest one of many. So a thorough and painstaking background check becomes a necessity. As part of the homework their motives too must be examined. Make sure your distributor or agent is thoroughly committed to actively working and collaborating with you. It makes sense therefore to start off in small steps to gauge their capability and performance. Make sure what you are promised is delivered. It is also important to be aware that, as in many developing countries, it is difficult and costly to dissolve a business relationship—and many have ended up acrimoniously in recent years. The *Doing Business 2011 Report* lists that it takes tremendous time to close a business in India based on its 134th ranking out of 183 countries surveyed. Any agreement should also include steps to be taken when either party wishes to exit from the partnership.[8]

Ensuring that a conflict of interest does not arise is paramount in any decision to appoint an agent or distributor and even more so when entering into a joint venture or equity-based relationship. There may be a conflict of interest when the potential agent handles similar product lines and many do. It is best to decide up-front if this is acceptable to avoid all kinds of issues and problems later on. The general rule of thumb of not putting all one's eggs in one basket hold true especially for businesses that have different operations. It is prudent to choose different partners instead of letting the same partner oversee the whole set of operations. This is to reduce dependency and to provide contingency support in the event of a conflict that might create costly and unnecessary bottlenecks that could have been prevented. Outline your expectations clearly and ensure that they are understood and accepted. Another related component of significance is to define the level of overall authority in appointing diligent key personnel to run the business in accordance with the overall strategic purpose. Control mechanisms must be established and execution must be easy. Strong control mechanisms minimize operational risks so that symptoms can be detected at an early stage for immediate rectification.[9] To succeed in India, both partners must understand each other's culture and be willing to accommodate the differences that are bound to arise. The risk of cultural integration can be mitigated by making special efforts in selecting the right partner and subsequently working tirelessly to build and maintain the relationship.

Negotiation Strategies for Optimum Results

In India every transaction is negotiated - every purchase, every payment, even marriages. Bargaining is a way of life in India. Hotmail founder Sabeer Bhatia, a California transplant from Bangalore, credits the bargaining skills he learned in vegetable markets at home for getting Microsoft to push its acquisition price for his company from $160 million to $400 million.[10] It would be an understatement to say that Indians are keen negotiators - they are known to be well prepared with data on competitive scenarios and prices. Their culture produces an uncommon blend of innovative thinking, business-minded aggression, and comfort with numbers. They should not be underestimated. The Indian has been described as a "complex, highly imaginative individual."[11]

The boss is very definitely the boss in India and as such negotiations must be held at the highest level. Decision-making is centralized at the top in organizational structures both public and private. Hierarchy is unquestionably accepted and decisions are always made at the highest level. Middle managers are generally not allowed to make decisions although they may steer proposals and give advice about them. Thus it makes sense to liaise as near to the top as possible. If dealing with the middle, it is best to seek out individuals who have some influence over the actual decision maker. Actual discussions and meetings are usually long-drawn affairs. Warm, cordial, and informal discussions are preferred and often include socialization over lunch and dinner. The Indian approach to negotiation is likely to be very indirect and ambiguous, though they can be direct when they are confident they are right and know what they want. As part of their culture they are bound to show much respect to the other party. Expect many distractions and interruptions during meetings and conversations, which may often be about unrelated issues. Engaging in small talk is the tradition in India and they spend considerable time in making you feel comfortable. Do not be frustrated over these rituals and practices or dismiss them as unnecessary or a waste of time.

Negotiations in India can be very slow and protracted compared with the West. They do not enjoy being hurried and have a subjective value of time. Indian culture promotes respecting and pleasing people. They will go out of their way to avoid confrontation and be more accommodating than others. Yet, they will be well prepared for the negotiations, having collected data on competitive scenarios and prices from their networks.[12] Expect them to bargain hard and have high expectations knowing fully well what they want. They will negotiate for weeks trying to get the best deal and eventually tire you into giving up the last 5%. The length of the process can be very unsettling to Westerners who "view time as money and would like to move on to the next project."[13] They think long-term and take time to understand the logic: competitive advantages, motivating forces, and in some instances "the spiritual timing or location of a business deal."[14] In Indian culture, timing is of utmost importance and certain days and times are considered "auspicious" for initiating projects or signing contracts.

Indian negotiators never give a straight "no" because they consider it impolite and disrespectful to do so. Instead they evade the issue, use the expressions "we'll see" or "we'll try," or try to prolong the negotiations. Polite nods and smiles do not signal agreement. Indians often sway their head from right to left which does not have a negative meaning but indicates that they understand what is being said; it must not be interpreted either as a sign of consent or approval. When they say "yes" it would be only to say that they heard what you say and not that they agree with you or accept your proposal. Open disagreement is rarely shown and harmony in the process is essential for successful negotiation. The use of aggressive tactics, confrontation, or pressurizing to reach a decision is counterproductive. Should a dispute arise it is recommended that a resolution be sought using friendliness, respect, and willingness to compromise.[15] Indians tend to be very emotional and being sensitive to their concerns will be of great help. Avoid arguments and use slow persuasive reasoning.

The most important areas to protect in any business agreement are security and confidentiality, legal compliance, fees and payment terms, proprietary rights, auditing rights, and dispute resolution process. Contractual obligations do not have the same sanctity in the Indian context as they do in Western culture. Indians have a preference for open-ended obligations as this gives them the flexibility to deal with changes in circumstances. Tying down the Indian party to very specific requirements may not yield much success and the use of general principles and guidelines may be more meaningful. Indian negotiators also often seek to take the moral high ground, which may lack pragmatism. They tend also to be very nationalistic and this is a natural response based on their past experience of having been dominated by foreigners for centuries. They can be very sensitive to actions by foreigners that they view as being detrimental to their country's well-being. The perceptions of Indians are also different - while in the West equity is based mostly on proportionality, in India it is more need-based. "There is the implicit expectation that the partner that is wealthier should make greater concessions."[16]

CHAPTER 5

Epilogue: India in Transition

India is a country in transition. The most widely noticed metamorphosis is economic. Reuters reported in 2012 that over the last 10 years, India's GDP has grown at an average of 7–9% per year, second only to China. Just this year, Forbes counted 57 Indian billionaires, up from only four a decade ago. "The same period saw Indian corporations vaulting onto the international stage. Tata Motors shocked the automobile industry with the acquisition of British Jaguar Land Rover business in 2008. India's famed BPO industry has expanded beyond call centers and software development to medicine, law, tax preparation, animation, and even music video production. And, several IT giants have turned the tables on offshoring: No longer are jobs only 'Bangalored.' Today, Indian companies employ thousands of Americans on US soil."[1]

India's share of global trade tripled between 1993 and 2010. The country has diversified rather well and managed to weather the global financial crisis in 2008 better than many emerging economies. The public debt situation in India is considerably better than many of the advanced countries in the world. In case of the EU, public debt was 80% of GDP during 2010. For some countries the public debt to GDP ratio was well over 100% (143% for Greece, 119% for Italy). For a large number of countries (including the United Kingdom, Germany, and France) this public debt to GDP ratio was in the range of 80–90%, while that of the United States was 96% in 2010. The situation in India is quite in contrast with fiscal deficit only 6.3% of GDP in 2010. The average fiscal deficit in the country for the last seven years has been around 4%. There is thus huge scope in India of augmenting public investment and thereby generating employment opportunities.

Despite the tremendous growth much needs to be done. Although on paper India is a thriving democracy, its governance has resembled something of a feudal system in practice. "Politicians and bureaucrats act often like dukes and barons with term limits. They routinely apply a corrupt layer of graft for their personal benefit."[2] An angry middle class is demanding change. An anti-corruption movement forced the Lok Sabha to pass the *Jan Lokpal Bill 2011* (anti-corruption Ombudsman law). The demand for change saw the end of 34 years of communist rule in West Bengal. Though poverty has been declining, half a billion still live on less than $2 a day. Literacy remains low and stands in the way of meaningful social mobility. Discrimination by caste, religion, and gender remains. The population of Indian cities, already more than 340 million, is projected to reach nearly 600 million by 2030.

The Economist Intelligence Unit[3] aptly sums up the risks of doing business in India (See Figure 5.1). It does not expect a surge in liberalization of economic reforms as things move very slowly in India. The legal system is relatively impartial but suffers from delays. The main risks to the economic outlook are the dangers posed by the large fiscal deficit and the high rate of inflation. The tax system is complex, although efforts are

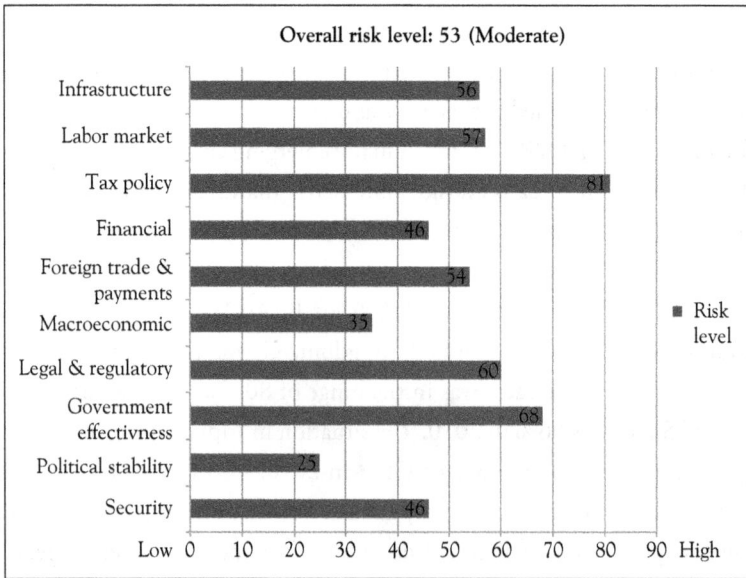

Figure 5.1. India overall risk level.

Source: Adapted from Business without Borders, Country Briefing 2011c (data compiled from Global Opportunity Tool, 2011). Retrieved on February 14, 2012, from: http://gotool. businesswithoutborders.com/CountryBriefing/?country=IN

underway to improve it. The labor market is highly regulated. Poor transport infrastructure can be a deterrent to investment.

India remains both a challenge and an opportunity. The country has fully embraced free-market capitalism but the resultant benefits are yet to be realized by many. Still, there is light at the end of the tunnel. Human and infrastructure development has been made a national priority. According to the World Bank, India's inequality (0.37) is still lower than that of China (0.42), the US (0.45) and Brazil (0.54) on the Gini coefficient. The Indian economy has balanced sources of growth with strong domestic demand, offering protection from external shocks. The conclusion can only be that India certainly has the potential but doing business is far from easy. One should expect the road to be long and winding but the results will be worth the effort. Patience, long-term orientation, adaptation, and perseverance remain the key to success in India.

CHAPTER 6

Web Resources

Background

Know India
http://india.gov.in/knowindia/profile.php

India and the World
http://india.gov.in/knowindia/india_world.php

India Culture and Heritage
http://india.gov.in/knowindia/culture_heritage.php

India Health
http://india.gov.in/citizen/health/health.php

India Ministry of Consumer Affairs, Food and Public Distribution
http://fcamin.nic.in/

India Ministry of Health and Family Welfare
http://mohfw.nic.in/

India Ministry of Home Affairs
http://mha.gov.in/

India Ministry of Labour
http://india.gov.in/outerwin.php?id=http://labour.nic.in/

India Ministry of Social Justice and Empowerment
http://socialjustice.nic.in/

India Ministry of Tourism
http://tourism.gov.in/

My India My Pride
http://india.gov.in/myindia/myindia.php

Government

Authority for Advance Rulings (part of the Central Board of Direct Taxes)
http://www.aar.gov.in/

Board for Industrial and Financial Reconstruction (BIFR)
http://www.bifr.nic.in

Bureau of Indian Standards (BIS)
http://www.bis.org.in

Central Board of Direct Taxes (CBDT), Income Tax Department, Department of Revenue, Ministry of Finance
http://incometaxindia.gov.in/ccit/CBDT.asp

Central Board of Excise and Customs (CBEC)
http://www.cbec.gov.in

Central Pollution Control Board, Ministry of Environment and Forests
http://www.cpcb.nic.in

Company Law Board
http://www.clb.nic.in

Competition Commission of India (CCI)
http://www.cci.gov.in

Constitution of India
http://india.gov.in/govt/constitutions_india.php

Controller of Certifying Authorities (CCA)
http://www.cca.gov.in

Copyright Office, Copyright division
http://www.copyright.gov.in

Directorate-General of Foreign Trade (DGFT), Ministry of Commerce and Industry:

http://dgft.gov.in

Export Credit Guarantee Corp (ECGC)
https://www.ecgc.in/Portal/Welcome.aspx

Export-Import Bank of India (Exim Bank)
http://www.eximbankindia.com

Foreign Investment Promotion Board (FIPB)
http://www.fipbindia.com

India Department of Heavy Industries
http://dhi.nic.in/

India Department of Higher Education
http://education.nic.in/secondary.htm

India Department of Information Technology
http://www.mit.gov.in/

India Department of Public Enterprises
http://dpe.nic.in/

India Department of School Education and Literacy
http://education.nic.in/Elementary/elementary.asp

India Department of Telecommunications
http://www.dot.gov.in/

India Economy
http://business.gov.in/indian_economy/index.php

India Ministry of Agriculture
http://agricoop.nic.in/

India Ministry of Defence
http://india.gov.in/sectors/defence/ministry_defence.php

India Ministry of Science and Technology
http://india.gov.in/sectors/science/ministry_science.php

India Ministry of Petroleum and Natural Gas
http://petroleum.nic.in/

India Ministry of Power
http://powermin.nic.in/

India Ministry of Railways
http://www.indianrailways.gov.in/

India Ministry of Road Transport and Highways
http://morth.nic.in/

India Ministry of Rural Development
http://rural.nic.in/

India Ministry of Urban Development
http://urbanindia.nic.in/

India National Informatics Center
http://www.nic.in/

Indian Investment Centre (IIC), Office of the Chief Commissioner (Investments and NRIs), Ministry of Finance
http://www.iic.nic.in

Know India
http://india.gov.in/knowindia/local_govt.php

Maps of India
http://www.mapsofindia.com/government-of-india/local/

Secretariat for Industrial Assistance (SIA), Department of Industrial Policy and Promotion, Ministry of Commerce and Industry

http:/www.dipp.gov.in

Institutions: International, NGOs, Trade Associations, Media

International Institutions

Asian Development Bank
http://beta.adb.org/countries/india/main

Codex India
http://codexindia.nic.in/

Food and Agriculture Organization of the United Nations
http://www.fao.org/countryprofiles/index.asp?x=3&y=5&iso3=IND

International Finance Corporation
*http://www1.ifc.org/wps/wcm/connect/region__ext_content/regions/
south+asia*

International Labor Organization
http://www.ilo.org/newdelhi/lang--en/index.htm

Organization for Economic Cooperation and Development
http://www.oecd.org/home/0,2987,en_2649_201185_1_1_1_1_1,00.html

The World Bank
http://www.worldbank.org/

The World Health Organization
http://www.searo.who.int/

Transparency International
http://www.transparency.org/

World Food Program
http://www.wfp.org/countries/india

World Travel and Tourist Council
http://www.wttc.org/

Non-Government Organizations

NGOs India
http://www.ngosindia.com/

Trade Associations

Associated Chambers of Commerce and Industry of India (Assocham)
http://www.assocham.org

Confederation of Indian Industries (CII)
http://www.ciionline.org

Federation of Indian Chambers of Commerce and Industry (FICCI)
http://www.ficci.com

Indian Chamber of Commerce
http://www.indianchamber.org/

Indo-American Chamber of Commerce
http://www.iaccindia.com

Indo-German Chamber of Commerce
http://www.indo-german.com

Media

DNA India
http://www.dnaindia.com/

Doordarshan
http://www.ddinews.gov.in/

Hindustan Times
http://www.hindustantimes.com/

New Delhi Television
http://www.ndtv.com/

Reuters India
http://in.reuters.com/

The Asian Age
http://www.asianage.com/

The Hindu
http://www.thehindu.com/

The Indian Express
http://www.indianexpress.com/

The Telegraph India
http://www.telegraphindia.com/section/frontpage/index.jsp

The Times of India
http://timesofindia.indiatimes.com/

The Tribune
http://www.tribuneindia.com/

Zee News
http://zeenews.india.com/

Business and Trade Practices

India Business Knowledge Resource
http://business.gov.in/

India Department of Commerce
http://commerce.nic.in/

India Department of Industrial Policy and Promotion
http://dipp.gov.in/English/default.aspx

India Department of Information Technology
http://www.mit.gov.in/

India Department of Telecommunications
http://www.dot.gov.in/

India Ministry of Corporate Affairs
http://www.mca.gov.in/

India Ministry of External Affairs
http://www.mea.gov.in/

India Ministry of Finance
http://mof.gov.in/

India Ministry of Labour and Employment
http://labour.gov.in/

India Ministry of Law and Justice
http://lawmin.nic.in/

India Ministry of Micro, Small and Medium Enterprises
http://msme.gov.in/

India Ministry of Statistics and Programme Implementation
http://mospi.nic.in/Mospi_New/site/home.aspx

Invest India
http://india.gov.in/outerwin.php?id=http://www.investindia.gov.in/

Patent Office
http://www.ipindia.nic.in/ipr/patent/patents.htm

Partner Search
http://www.expandinindia.net/business-partners.php

Set up business in India
http://singularity.in/services/setup-business-india/

Registrar of Trademarks
http://www.ipindia.nic.in/tmr_new/default.htm

Reserve Bank of India (RBI)
http://www.rbi.org.in

Notes

Chapter 1

1. Yardley (2011).
2. Diamond (1999).
3. Diamond (1999).
4. Bhasin (2007).
5. Central Intelligence Agency (2011).
6. Library of Congress (2004).
7. Central Intelligence Agency (2011).
8. Library of Congress (2004).
9. Central Intelligence Agency (2011).
10. U.S. Department of State (2010).
11. Library of Congress (2004).
12. U.S. Department of State (2010).
13. U.S. Department of State (2010).
14. U.S. Department of State (2010).
15. Central Intelligence Agency (2011).
16. U.S. Department of State (2010).
17. Library of Congress (2004).
18. Library of Congress (2004).
19. Library of Congress (2004).
20. Bhasin (2007).
21. Library of Congress (2004).

Chapter 2

1. Government of India (2011).
2. Government of India (2011).
3. Government of India (2011) and U.S. Commercial Service (2011).
4. U.S. Commercial Service (2011).
5. U.S. Commercial Service (2011).
6. U.S. Commercial Service (2011).
7. Government of India (2011) and U.S. Commercial Service (2011).
8. Shrivastawa (2011).
9. U.S. Commercial Service (2011).
10. U.S. Commercial Service (2011).

11. Government of India (2011).
12. India Brand Equity Foundation (2011).
13. Government of India (2011).
14. Vora (2012).
15. India Brand Equity Foundation (2011).
16. Report for Congress (2007).
17. UK Trade and Investment (2011).
18. Deboy et al. (2011).
19. The World Bank (2011).
20. Maple & Cians (2010).
21. McKinsey (2007).
22. Bharadwaj (2005).
23. Kearny (2011).
24. The Economic Times (2011).
25. Yardley and Bajaj (2011).
26. McKinsey (2007).
27. Indian Retail Report (2009).
28. Shukla (2009).
29. McKinsey (2007).
30. Deutsche Bank Research (2010).
31. McKinsey (2007).
32. Wikipedia (2011).
33. Prahalad and Stuart (2002).
34. Maple & Cians (2010).
35. The World Bank (2011c).
36. Green World Investor (2011).
37. Overdorf (2009).
38. The World Bank (2011b).
39. National Association of Software and Services Companies (2009).
40. Baldia (2007).
41. Baldia (2007).
42. Times of India (2011).
43. Sauvant (2011).
44. India Brand Equity Foundation (2011).
45. Sauvant (2011).
46. India Brand Equity Foundation (n.d.).
47. Organization for Economic Corporation and Development (2009).
48. KPMG (2010).
49. The Economist (2011).
50. KPMG (2010).
51. The Economist (2011).
52. India Brand Equity Foundation.

53. Leaver (2009).
54. The Economist (2011).
55. Yardley and Bajaj (2011).
56. Leaver (2009).
57. The Economist (2011).

Chapter 3

1.   The World Bank (2012).
2.   Sridharan (2008).
3.   Hindustan Times (2011).
4.   A.M. Best Report (2011).
5.   Chaulia (2010).
6.   Babus of India (2010).
7.   India Times (2012).
8.   Glekin and Dixon (2012).
9.   Stancati (2011).
10. The Economist (2011).
11. Global Advice Network (2011).
12. The Hindu (2011).
13. The World Bank (2012).
14. Dhara (2011).
15. Taxation News (2012).
16. The World Bank (2012).
17. U.S. Commercial Service (2011).
18. Chandrasekhar (2010).
19. Deshgujarat (2011).
20. Pearson (2011).
21. Federation of Indian Chamber of Commerce and Industry (2011).
22. Government of India (2010).
23. Sethi (2011).
24. Bajaj (2011).
25. Sinha (2010).
26. Bose (2011).
27. Yardley (2011).
28. Basu (2007).
29. MacAskill and Mehrotra (2011).
30. India Today (2011).
31. Times of India (2012).
32. India Today (2011).
33. Kumar (2011).

Chapter 4

1. Sinha and Kumar (2004).
2. Sinha and Kumar (2004).
3. Sinha and Kumar (2004).
4. Kumar (2005).
5. Kumar (2005).
6. Sinha and Kumar (2004).
7. Bhasin (2007).
8. The Metropolitan Corporate Counsel (2011).
9. Gupta and Wang (2010).
10. Ferriss (2007).
11. Kumar (2005).
12. Stetson-Rodriguez (2007).
13. Kumar (2005).
14. Stetson-Rodriguez (2007).
15. Katz (2008).
16. Kumar (2005).

Chapter 5

1. Toyama (2012).
2. Toyama (2012).
3. Economic Intelligence Unit (2011).

References

Best, A. M. (2011). *AMB country risk report: India A.M. best ratings and analysis center,* N.J. Retrieved January 17, 2012, from: http://www3.ambest.com/ratings/cr/reports/India.pdf

Babus of India. (2010). BoI survey on Indian bureaucracy gives fractured verdict. Retrieved January 27, 2012, from: http://www.babusofindia.com/2010/06/boi-survey-on-indian-bureaucracy-gives.html

Bajaj, V. (2011, November 30). Outsourcing giant finds it must be client too. *The New York Times.*

Baldia, S. (2007). Thinking outside the BPO: Knowledge process outsourcing to India" *Business & technology sourcing and India practice groups at Mayer, Brown, Rowe & Maw,* Washington DC. November, 2007. Retrieved January 7, 2012, from: http://www.mayerbrown.com/publications/article.asp?id=3534&nid=6

Basu, I. (2007, January 5). India's mushrooming black economy. *Asia Times Online.*

BBC News. (2011). India income inequality doubles in 20 years, says OECD. Retrieved January 3, 2012, from: http://www.bbc.co.uk/news/world-asia-india-16064321

Bharadwaj, V. T., Swaroop, G. M., & Vittal, I. (2005). "Winning the Indian consumer", *McKinsey Quarterly,* McKinsey and Company, New York, September 2005. Retrieved December 28, 2011, from: https://www.mckinseyquarterly.com/Winning_the_Indian_consumer_1659

Bhasin, B. (2007). Succeeding in China: Cultural adjustments for Indian businesses. *Journal of Cross Cultural Management 14*(1), 43–53.

Bose, A. (2011). Without black money, India can be a $9 tn economy. Retrieved February 5, 2012, from: http://www.firstpost.com/economy/without-black-money-india-can-be-a-9-tn-economy-74539.html

Business without Borders. (2011a). *Global opportunity tool.* Retrieved February 14, 2012, from: http://gotool.businesswithoutborders.com/CountryBriefing/?country=IN

Business without Borders. (2011b). *Global opportunity tool.* Retrieved February 14, 2012, from: http://country.eiu.com/article.aspx?articleid=1038359288&Country=India&topic=Economy&subtopic=Long-term+outlook&subsubtopic=India--highlights%3a+Long-term+outlook

Business without Borders. (2011c). *Global opportunity tool.* Retrieved February 25, 2012, from: http://country.eiu.com/article.aspx?articleid=218773406&Country=India&topic=Summary&subtopic=Fact+sheet&subsubtopic=Fact+sheet

Central Intelligence Agency. (2011). *The world factbook.* Retrieved December 19, 2011, from: https://www.cia.gov/library/publications/the-world-factbook/geos/in.html

Chaulia, S. (2010, June 10). Byzantine bureaucracy. *The Financial Express.*

Cohen, R. (1997). *Negotiating across cultures: Communication obstacles in international diplomacy.* Washington DC: US Institute of Peace.

Confederation of Indian Industry, (CII) & Kearney, A. T. (2011). India luxury review 2011. Retrieved October 13, 2011, from: http://www.atkearney.in/images/india/pdf/India-Luxury-Review-2011-CII-AT-Kearney-Report.pdf

Das, G. (2001, June 3). Indian paradoxes. *Times of India.*

Debroy, B., Bhandari, L., & Aiyar S. S. A. (2011). *Economic freedom of states of India, 2011.* New Delhi: Academic Foundation.

Deshgujarat. (2011). Ninety four percent of India's total labor force is in the unorganized sector. Retrieved February 4, 2012, from: http://deshgujarat.com

Deutsche Bank Research. (2010). The middle class in India. Retrieved January 3, 2012, from: http://www.dbresearch.de/PROD/DBR_INTERNET_EN-PROD/PROD0000000000253735.pdf

Dhara, T., & Thomas, C. (2011, July 28). In India, tax evasion is a national sport. *Bloomberg Businessweek.*

Diamond, J. (1999). *Guns, germs and steel: The fates of human societies.* New York, NY: W.W. Norton and Company.

Economic Intelligence Unit. (2011, February). Overall risk assessment – India. *The Economist.*

Ernst & Young. (2010). *Doing business in India.* Gurgaon, India: Ernst & Young Private Limited.

Federation of Indian Chamber of Commerce and Industry. (2011). FICCI survey on labor/skill shortage for industry. Retrieved February 4, 2012, from: http://www.ficci.com/SEDocument/20165/FICCI_Labour_Survey.pdf

Ferriss, T. (2007). *How to negotiate like an Indian — 7 Rules.* Retrieved February 25, 2012, from: http://www.fourhourworkweek.com/blog/2007/12/11/how-to-negotiate-like-an-indian-7-rules/

Glekin, J., & Dixon, H. (2012, January 18). Unraveling India, *Reuters.*

Global Advice Network. (2011). *Business anti-corruption portal. India judicial system.* Retrieved January 30, 2012, from: http://www.business-anti-corruption.com/country-profiles/south-asia/india/corruption-levels/judicial-system/

Global Peace Index. (2011).*Vision of humanity.* Retrieved January 17, 2012, from: http://www.visionofhumanity.org/gpi-data/#/2011/scor

Government of India. (2010, July 1). Annual report to the people on employment. *Ministry of Labor and Employment.*

Government of India. (2011). Economic survey 2010–2011. *Ministry of finance,* New Delhi. Retrieved December 19, 2011, from: http://indiabudget.nic.in/index.asp

Green World Investor. (2011). *India's shocking income inequality – 50 billionaires and 800 million desperately poor*. Retrieved January 8, 2012, from: http://www.greenworldinvestor.com/2011/03/10/indias-shocking-income-inequality-50-billionaires-and-800-million-desperately-poor/

Gupta, A. K., & Wang, H. (2010). *How to avoid getting burned in China and India*. Retrieved October 7, 2011, from: http://www.businessweek.com/globalbiz/content/mar2010/gb2010031_639418.htm

Hattari, R., & Rajan, R. S. (2010). India as a source of outward foreign direct investment. *Oxford Development Studies 38*(4), 497–518.

Hindustan Times. (2011). Less democracy better for India, says Mahathir. *Hindustan Times Leadership Summit*, December 2–3, 2011. Retrieved January 17, 2012, from: http://htsummit.hindustantimes.com/summit-news/less-democracy-better-for-india-says-mahathir.php

India Brand Equity Foundation (2011). India Knowledge Center. *Ministry of Commerce with the Confederation of Indian Industry (CII)*, India. Retrieved December 25, 2011, from: http://www.ibef.org/home.aspx

Indian Brand Equity Foundation. (n.d.). India's new opportunity – 2020. Retrieved January 9, 2012, from: http://www.ibef.org/download/IndiaNewOpportunity.pdf

India Times. (2012, January 11). Indian bureaucracy rated worst in Asia, says a Political & Economic Risk Consultancy report, *The Economic Times*, India Times.

India Today. (2011, October 20). Black money. Pranab Mukherjee says 9,900 Indian overseas accounts under probe. *India Today Magazine*.

Katz, L. (2008). Negotiating International Business – India. *Negotiating international business: The negotiator's reference guide to 50 countries around the world*, Booksurge Publishing March, 2008.

KPMG. (2010). *Resurgent PSUs. Vibrant India*. Retrieved January 8, 2012, from: http://www.kpmg.com/IN/en/IssuesAndInsights/ThoughtLeadership/KPMG_Resurgent_PSUs_Vibrant_India_ASSOCHAM.pdf

Kumar, A. (2011, August 20). The cost of the black economy. *The Hindu*.

Kumar, R. (2005). Negotiating with the complex, imaginative Indian. *Ivey Business Journal*, London, Ontario, Canada March/April 2005.

Library of Congress. (2004). Country profile: India. *Federal Research Division*, Washington, D.C. Retrieved on June 28, 2011, from: http://memory.loc.gov/frd/cs/profiles/India.pdf

MacAskill, A., & Mehrotra, K. (2011, June 16). Can India's power thieves be stopped?. *Bloomberg Businessweek*.

Maple Capital Advisors. (2010). *India consumer story*. Retrieved January 7, 2012, from: http://maple-advisors.com/Maple%20Capital%20Advisors%20-%20India%20Consumer%20Story.pdf

Mckinsey & Company. (2011). *The 'bird of gold': The rise of India's consumer market*. Retrieved January 7, 2012, from: http://www.mckinsey.com/Insights/MGI/Research/Asia/The_bird_of_gold

Nachiappan, Devi, & Kiran. (2008). *Family business management – Small and medium enterprises in Tamil Nadu.* Retrieved January 8, 2012, from: http://www.isb.edu/FamilyBusinessConference/FamilyBusinessManagement.pdf

NASSCOM. (2009). Perspective 2020. Transform Business, Transform India", *National Association of Software and Services Companies (NASSCOM)* and *McKinsey and Company,* New Delhi, April, 2009. Retrieved January 4, 2012, from: http://www.mckinsey.com/locations/india/mckinseyonindia/pdf/NASSCOM_report_exec_summ.pdf

Organization for Economic Co-operation and Development (OECD). (2009). *State owned enterprises in India: Reviewing the evidence.* Retrieved January 8, 2012, from: http://www.oecd.org/dataoecd/14/28/42095406.pdf

Overdorf, J. (2011). *Want to grow rich in India? Think poor.* Retrieved September 16, 2011 from: http://www.globalpost.com/dispatch/india/090813/indias-economy-grow-rich-think-poor

Pearson M., & Sharma, P. (2011, January 6). Where are India's skilled workers. *Bloomberg Businessweek.*

Prahalad, C. K., & Hart, S. L. (2002). *The fortune at the bottom of the pyramid.* Retrieved September 2, 2011, from: http://www.cs.berkeley.edu/~brewer/ict4b/Fortune-BoP.pdf

Report for Congress. (2007). India-US Economic Trade Relations. *Congressional Research Service,* Report for Congress Order Code RL 34161, Washington, D.C. August 31, 2007.

Sauvant, K. P., Govitrikar, V., & Davies, K. G. (2011). *MNEs from emerging markets: New players in the world FDI market.* New York: Vale Columbia Center.

Saxena, R. (2010). The middle class in India: Issues and opportunities. *Deutsche Bank Research,* February 15, 2010. Retrieved January 3, 2012, from: http://www.dbresearch.de/PROD/DBR_INTERNET_DE-PROD/PROD0000000000253735.pdf

Seth, A. (2011, November 10). India's more perfect union. *The New York Times.*

Shrivastava, A. (2011). The impact of FDI on India's manufacturing sector. *India Briefing,* February 11, 2011. Retrieved December 25, 2011, from: http://www.india-briefing.com/news/impact-fdi-indias-manufacturing-sector-4646.html/

Shukla, R. (2009). *Changing income demographics and its implication for marketers.* Retrieved January 8, 2012, from: http://www.ncaer.org/downloads/MediaClips/Press/RajeshShukla-Articles-India%20Retail%20report-2009.pdf

Shukla, R. (2011). *Income inequality has increased after 12 years of economic reform.* Retrieved September 29, 2011, from: http://www.ncaer.org/downloads/MediaClips/Press/RShuklaInclusionAprilJune2011.pdf

Sinha, P., & Singh, N. (2010, March 22). India loses Rs. 10 lakh crore from black economy every year. *Economic Times Bureau.*

Sinha, J. B. P., & Kumar, R. (2004). Methodology for understanding Indian culture. *The Copenhagen Journal of Asian Studies 19*, 89–104.

Sridharan, E. (2008). Coalition politics in India: Types, duration, theory and comparison. *Institute of South Asian Studies (ISAS)*, Singapore 2008. Retrieved January 16, 2012, from: http://www.isn.ethz.ch/isn/Digital-Library/Publications/Detail/?ots591=0C54E3B3-1E9C-BE1E-2C24-A6A8C7060233&lng=en&id=92186

Stancati, M. (2011, December 1). India Sinks Lower in Corruption Index. *The Wall Street Journal – India.*

Stetson-Rodriguez, M. (2007). *Negotiations and business strategies with India.* Retrieved February 25, 2012, from *Venture Outsource* on: http://www.ventureoutsource.com/contract-manufacturing/outsourcing-offshoring/india-manufacturing/negotiations-and-business-strategies-with-india

Taxation News and Information. (2011). *India delays GST until June 2012.* Retrieved January 31, 2012, from: http://www.taxationinfonews.com/2011/06/india-delays-gst-until-june-2012/

The Economic Times. (2011). *India has more rich households than most European nations.* Retrieved October 13, 2011, from: http://articles.economictimes.indiatimes.com/2011-10-08/news/30258141_1_tns-s-global-affluent-investor-tns-director-households

The Economist. (2011, March 10). "Corruption in India. A million rupees now.

The Economist. (2011). A weak state has given rise to a new kind of economy. Without reform, it will hit limits. Retrieved January 4, 2012, from: http://www.economist.com/node/21533396

The Economist. (2011). The bollygarch's magic mix. Retrieved October 26, 2011, from: http://www.economist.com/node/21532449

The Hindu. (2011). Reforms could see disposal of cases in three years. Retrieved January 30, 2012, from: http://www.thehindu.com/news/national/article2129739.ece

The Metropolitan Corporate Counsel. (2011). *Mutual benefits and big opportunities of doing business in India.* Retrieved February 7, 2012, from: http://www.metrocorpcounsel.com/pdf/2011/January/40.pdf

The World Bank. (2011a). *India economic update.* Retrieved January 7, 2012, from: http://www.worldbank.org.in/WBSITE/EXTERNAL/COUNTRIES/SOUTHASIAEXT/INDIAEXTN/0, contentMDK:23026570~pagePK:149 7618~piPK:217854~theSitePK:295584,00.html

The World Bank. (2011). *Doing Business in India, 2011.* Washington DC: The International Bank for Reconstruction and Development/The World Bank.

The World Bank. (2012). *Doing business 2012: Economy profile: India.* Washington DC: The International Bank for Reconstruction and Development/The World Bank.

The Worldbank. (2009). *Economy rankings India*. Retrieved January 7, 2012, from: http://www.doingbusiness.org/rankings/India/

The Worldbank. (2011b). *India economic update*. Retrieved January 7, 2012, from: http://www.worldbank.org.in/WBSITE/EXTERNAL/COUNTRIES/SOUTHASIAEXT/INDIAEXTN/0,contentMDK:22952327~menuPK:50003484~pagePK:2865066~piPK:2865079~theSitePK:295584,00.html

Times of India. (2011, June 23). Outward FDI by India Inc. hits $43 bn. *Times of India, New Delhi.*

Times of India. (2012, February 13). Black money. Indians have stashed over $500 bn in banks abroad, says CBI. *Times of India.*

Toyama, K. (2012, February 20). The two Indias: Astounding poverty in the backyard of amazing growth. *The Atlantic.*

U.S. Commercial Service. (2011). Doing business in India: 2011 country commercial guide for U.S. companies. *U.S. & Foreign Commercial Service and U.S. Department of State, 2011.* Retrieved December 19, 2011, from: http://www.buyusainfo.net/docs/x_2918659.pdf

U.S. Department of State. (2011). "Background note: India" *Bureau of South and Central Asian Affairs, U.S. Department of State, November 8, 2011.* Retrieved on December 19, 2011, from: http://www.state.gov/r/pa/ei/bgn/3454.htm

UK Trade and Investment. (2011). *Opportunities for London businesses in emerging cities of India.* London: UK Trade and Investment and UK-India Business Council.

Vora, S. (2012, February 13). Outsourcing's surprise by-product: More luxury hotels in India. *The New York Times.*

Wikipedia. (2012). *Bottom of the pyramid*. Retrieved January 7, 2012, from: http://en.wikipedia.org/wiki/Bottom_of_the_pyramid

World Economic Forum. (2011–2012). *The global competitiveness report, 2011–2012.* Retrieved February 18, 2012, from: http://gcr.weforum.org/gcr2011/

Yardley, J., & Bajaj, V. (2011). *Billionaires' rise aids India, and the favor is returned.* Retrieved September 2, 2011, from: http://www.nytimes.com/2011/07/27/world/asia/27tycoon.html

Yardley, J. (2011, June 8). In India, dynamism wrestles with dysfunction. *The New York Times.*

Yardley, J. (2011, December 29). India's second economy, in shadows and slums. *New York Times News Service.*

Index

Announcing the Business Expert Press Digital Library

Concise E-books Business Students Need for Classroom and Research

This book can also be purchased in an e-book collection by your library as

- a one-time purchase,
- that is owned forever,
- allows for simultaneous readers,
- has no restrictions on printing, and
- can be downloaded as PDFs from within the library community.

Our digital library collections are a great solution to beat the rising cost of textbooks. e-books can be loaded into their course management systems or onto student's e-book readers.

The **Business Expert Press** digital libraries are very affordable, with no obligation to buy in future years. For more information, please visit **www.businessexpertpress.com/librarians**. To set up a trial in the United States, please contact **Adam Chesler** at *adam.chesler@businessexpertpress. com* for all other regions, contact **Nicole Lee** at *nicole.lee@igroupnet.com*.

OTHER TITLES IN OUR INTERNATIONAL BUSINESS COLLECTION

Collection Editors: **Tamer Cavusgil, Michael R. Czinkota, Gary Knight**

- *Export Marketing Strategy: Tactics and Skills that Work* by Tamer Cavusgil, Shaoming Zou and Daekwan Kim
- *Born Global Firms: A New International Enterprise* by Gary Knight and Tamer Cavusgil
- *Conducting Market Research for International Business* by Tamer Cavusgil, Gary Knight, John Riesenberger and Attila Yaprak
- *Emerging Trends, Threats and Opportunities in International Marketing: What Executives Need to Know* by Michael R. Czinkota, Ilkka Ronkainen and Masaaki Kotabe
- *The Internationalists: Masters of the Global Game* by Catherine Scherer
- *Managing International Business in Relation-Based Versus Rule-Based Countries* by Shaomin Li
- *International Social Entrepreneurship* by Joseph Mark Munoz
- *Doing Business in the ASEAN Countries* by Balbir Bhasin
- *Successful Cross-Cultural Management: A Guidebook for International Managers* by Parissa Haghirian
- *Understanding Japanese Management Practices* by Parissa Hagihirian
- *A Strategic and Tactical Approach to Global Business Ethics* by Lawrence A. Beer
- *China: Doing Business in the Middle Kingdom* by Stuart C. Strother
- *Global Business Negotiations* by Claude Cellich and Subhash C. Jain

www.ingramcontent.com/pod-product-compliance
Lightning Source LLC
Chambersburg PA
CBHW071155200326
41519CB00018B/5235